George Santayana, Literary Philosopher

Books by Irving Singer

George Santayana, Literary Philosopher

Reality Transformed: Film as Meaning and Technique

Meaning in Life

The Creation of Value

The Pursuit of Love

The Harmony of Nature and Spirit

The Nature of Love

Plato to Luther

Courtly and Romantic

The Modern World

Mozart and Beethoven: The Concept of Love in Their Operas

The Goals of Human Sexuality

Santayana's Aesthetics

Essays in Literary Criticism by George Santayana (editor)

The Nature and Pursuit of Love: The Philosophy

of Irving Singer (edited by David Goicoechea)

George Santayana, Literary Philosopher

Irving Singer

Yale University Press   New Haven & London

Designed by Rebecca Gibb.
Set in Bembo type by The Composing Room of Michigan, Inc.
Printed in the United States of America
by Vail-Ballou Press, Binghamton, New York.

Library of Congress Cataloging-in-Publication Data

Singer, Irving.
　　George Santayana, literary philosopher / Irving Singer.
　　　　p.　cm.
　　Includes bibliographical references (p.　) and index.
　　ISBN 0-300-08037-9 (cloth : alk. paper)
　　　1. Santayana, George, 1863–1952.　I. Title.
　　B945.S24 S56 2000
　　191—dc21　　　　　　　　　　　　　　　　99-053686

A catalogue record for this book is available from the British Library.

The paper in this book meets the guidelines for permanence and durability of
the Committee on Production Guidelines for Book Longevity of the Council
on Library Resources.

10 9 8 7 6 5 4 3 2 1

To the memory of Walter Jackson Bate and Henry David Aiken

Contents

Preface

WHEN I WAS YOUNG, the American philosopher who meant the most to me was John Dewey. During my early years, which co-incided with the Depression and World War II, Dewey represented most of what I believed in at the time: naturalism, humanism, demo-cratic pluralism, pragmatism as the clue to knowledge. I felt that he, better than any other philosopher I had read, understood the goodness of a healthy-minded life that combines the best in science and in art. My undergraduate honors thesis on Dewey's theory of value was a sympathetic, though somewhat critical, attempt to extend his fundamental orientation beyond the limits he had set. I never thought of myself as a disciple, and Dewey's impoverished literary style often made me cringe. Nevertheless, I saw him as a model of how an intellectual could also be an active force in society, efficacious through his writing as well as through his devotion to liberal causes that mattered greatly to me.

As the years went by, I gravitated more and more toward the work of George Santayana. I wrote my graduate dissertation on his aesthetics, which seemed to me more challenging and possibly more fertile than Dewey's. I later realized that, among philosophers trained in the Anglo-Saxon traditions of the nineteenth and twentieth centuries, only Santayana had exhaustively investigated the questions about love that increasingly interested me—questions about love as a topic in philosophy as well as a theme in literature and all the other arts. From the start, I considered Santayana's Neoplatonism a serious impediment in his official outlook. But since I had always loved the dialogues of Plato as supreme examples of literature no less than philosophy, I was fascinated by Santayana's merging of a twentieth-century version of Platonism with an up-to-date materialism to which he gave equal importance.

Relying on Dewey as my touchstone for a wholesome, balanced, and defensible alternative to both Platonistic idealism and reductivist materialism, I found myself in the anomalous position of repudiating Santayana's doctrine while also relishing his resplendent construction of it. Though I concluded that his attempt to unify Platonism and naturalism fails as philosophy, I felt then, and always have, that it succeeds as an exciting and uniquely inspirational expression of humanistic imagination. Santayana was what the Spanish call a *pensador*, a thinker in the broadest sense, whose books were filled with rich aperçus and wise inventiveness. I found his thinking closer to actual experience than any other contemporary philosophy in the English language. His prose glittered and was burnished in a manner that invited emulation at whatever level I myself might someday attain.

I was additionally attracted to Santayana's approach by the fact that it encompasses persistent modes of alienation recurrent in his own experience but characteristic of the world as I knew it too. Santayana was both an insider and an outsider in American life. Although he resided in the United States for more than forty years, he remained until he died a European man of letters and a Spanish citizen. Throughout his life he was a Catholic and an atheist, a scholar and an author addressing the intelligent public at large, a man who saw the world as many other Spaniards did but one whose works were written in English, a technical philosopher as well as a poet, critic, novelist, and cultural historian, a product of his time yet never at home in it. He was all these as they enacted a permanent counterpoint of divisions within himself. I was not divided in the same way as he, but his example helped me to see the extent to which I was alienated as well. If the benign and consummate activism of Dewey proferred an ideal that I might contemplate at a distance, study of the problematics of Santayana's philosophy showed me the residual rifts that my kind of person would have to face up to sooner or later. Dewey could never have elicited that awareness in me.

A few years ago I was asked to participate in a documentary about Santayana's life and work, to be directed toward teen-age Hispanics in America. At first I thought that the project was utterly unrealistic. How many young people nowadays, regardless of their ethnic origin, would even have heard of Santayana? How many of them would want to know about anything he had published? But then it occurred to me that this venture could serve a useful purpose. Most of the students who would watch the video were also alienated from their American surroundings. Not entirely but to a large degree, they experienced many of the inner divisions that

Santayana underwent. The young Hispanics might never read much of what he wrote, but they could easily appreciate the nature of his situation as a human being. Learning that he survived, even flourished, through faith in his capacity to surmount his alienated condition, to transform it creatively by works of individual talent that his imagination made available to him, they might intuit a comparable solution for themselves. Whether or not the video would actually attain this goal, I was happy to participate in it after all.[1]

This book may be taken as a similar attempt. It is an introduction to the part of Santayana's philosophy that has meant the most to me. Though it begins with an account of my first acquaintance with his thought, and my visit to him in Rome, it is a portrayal of his lasting achievement from the perspective of its humanistic relevance. It concentrates on problems about the nature of art, criticism, love, and the good life as Santayana formulated them in his books. Over the years my own writing as a literary philosopher was frequently inspired by developments in Santayana's approach, even when I did not agree with them. The present book is a study of those developments, together with my reaction and running commentary.

I have considerably revised or rewritten most of the material in the text that originally appeared on other occasions. The sources are documented in the endnotes, but here I wish to remark that my discussion of Daniel Cory's biography in Chapter 2 had a different title when its earlier version was published in *The New York Review of Books*. Without my foreknowledge, the editors of that journal attached a heading that I consider pejorative to Santayana's genius. They entitled the piece "Marble Faun." While this allusion to Hawthorne's novel about American expatriates in Europe is accurate and suggestive in various ways, it intimates a type of feckless, even effete, aestheticism that is grossly untrue to the mature wisdom that Santayana acquired and expressed in his later years.

In retaining its focus upon Santayana's humanistic philosophy, the book cites but scarcely discusses many important publications by other Santayana specialists. Since the Santayana Society came into existence twenty years ago, much has been written that is worthy of detailed attention. I hope such promising research will get the professional recognition it deserves. Though my work is designed for a more general audience, it also seeks to find a niche within that vital area of scholarship.

Among the many people who have aided and abetted the completion of this book, in one way or another, I am particularly grateful to the following persons: James Engell, Cayetano Estébanez, Cándido Pérez Gállego, Carmen García-Trevijano, Manuel Garrido, Morris Grossman, Felipe Guardiola, José Antonio Gurpegui, Henry Hardy, Larisa Heimert, Angus Kerr-Lawson, Paul Grimley Kuntz, Richard A. Macksey, Timothy J. Madigan, Frederick Morgan, Joel Porte, Manuel Villar Raso, José M. Ruiz Ruiz, Herman J. Saatkamp, Jr., Michael Shinagel, Jo Singer, David Wapinsky, and David F. Wheeler.

George Santayana, Literary Philosopher

1   A Pilgrimage to Santayana

WHEN HISTORIANS in the twenty-first century assess the nature of twentieth-century philosophy from their own perspective, they may have some difficulty in placing the mind and works of George Santayana. There are two ways in which we might appraise his contribution. We could take him as a writer about the human condition who also did philosophy; or else as a theorist in various branches of philosophy who wrote essays, literary criticism, history of ideas, social commentary, volumes of poetry, a best-selling novel, and so on. Both approaches to his talent must be employed, and interwoven, in order to attain a clear idea of what Santayana accomplished in his books.

More than any other great philosopher in the English language, Santayana not only harmonized the two types of writing—the literary and the philosophical—but also made harmonization of this sort a fundamental resource in his doctrinal outlook. In the preface to *Scepticism and Animal Faith* he writes that if the reader is tempted to smile at the idea that he is offering "one more system of philosophy," he smiles as well.[1] Despite its systematic structure, Santayana's philosophy was intended to be an expression of the author's personal experience and imaginative interpretation of his life as he lived it. Neither in his works nor in anyone else's, he thought, could a reader find the certitude and objectivity that so many others promised.

In taking this attitude, Santayana believed that philosophical speculation was inherently a literary pursuit and therefore a branch of the humanities rather than of the sciences. Santayana sought to further humanistic acuities that would permeate philosophy as they also permeate fine arts and the various forms of criticism that interpret and evaluate them. He denied that these different facets of human inspiration could be reduced or rendered subservient to technical procedures that science (correctly) employs for its own expertise. He recognized that the life of the mind, above all in the humanities, becomes stunted when artificial barriers are reared between philosophy and literature or between philosophy and history or, in a different dimension, between creative and critical insights. Ideally these would not be separated from one another. To the extent that they establish a harmonious interpenetration, they enrich each other.

Above all in the United States, but now in most other countries, intellectual and academic fields have become increasingly splintered in the twentieth century, even split into hermetically distinct compartments. The long humanistic tradition that linked the early Renaissance to the art and history of the ancient world, and then continued to evolve for the next five hundred years, has suffered disabilities from which it may never recover. In the past few decades, the danger to the humanistic spirit has accelerated greatly. As a reminder of what we have had, and as a model for what we may yet regain as a supplement to the new achievements on which we can rightly pride ourselves, Santayana's books merit the renewed study that some scholars are now giving them. Though far from completed, the new critical edition of his works has already encouraged this return to Santayana and what he represents as a philosopher.[2]

In a book published in 1949, Somerset Maugham laments the fact that it was in the service of philosophy that Santayana used his "great gifts, gifts of imagery, of metaphor, of apt simile and of brilliant illustration." Maugham doubts that philosophy needs "the decoration of a luxuriance so lush." He regretfully concludes: "It was a loss to American literature when Santayana decided to become a philosopher rather than a novelist."[3]

In saying this, Maugham fails to recognize that Santayana's literary gifts were not employed for mere decoration, even when his prose was lush and luxuriant, but rather as the means by which he could express his view of the world in a way that transcends any preconceptions about what either literature or philosophy "ought" to be. Santayana's fusion of the two disciplines was an enrichment, not a loss, to both American philosophy and American literature.

Writing in 1937, John Crowe Ransom said: "Among philosophical personalities probably the most urbane and humanistic since Socrates is Mr. Santayana."[4] In one of his letters Santayana remarks: "In my old-fashioned terminology, a Humanist means a person saturated by the humanities: Humanism is something cultural: an accomplishment, not a doctrine."[5] In renouncing humanism as a doctrine, Santayana was asserting his usual belief that the imagination must never be constrained by any fixed or codified tenets. By serving as an accomplishment, humanism would illustrate the fact that virtually all areas of learning can find a home within the mentality of a person who is truly cultivated and radically enlightened. Santayana's writings themselves embody the highest aspirations of this humanistic faith, and throughout its subtle modulations his thought serves to buttress even the most diversified types of humanism.

Nevertheless, Santayana's philosophical novel *The Last Puritan* was generally neglected by professionals in literature as well as philosophy for almost sixty years after it was first published, and during most of that time there existed no inexpensive edition that English-language readers could readily acquire. For the most part Santayana's other works were ignored not only by the prevailing tendencies in contemporary thought but also by the popular culture. His ideas survived mainly in a few well-turned epigrams, such as the famous line (often misquoted) from *Reason in Common Sense:* "Those who cannot remember the past are condemned to repeat it."[6] These words were traced in large letters on a placard just behind the altar in Jonestown, Guyana. After the massacre they were visible in photographs of the site that appeared in newspapers. They were, in fact, the only text to be seen—like holy script wrenched out of context.

This desecration of Santayana's perceptiveness, and the unfriendliness toward his philosophy in academic circles, may yet be rectified. My hope is partly based on healthy changes that are now occurring. More than at any time since Santayana's death in 1952, work is being done in the kind of humanistic approach that Santayana favored. In various ways, though not massively as yet, American philosophy is returning to questions about the nature and quality of human experience, of living the good life, of creating or discovering values and expressing them in action as well as works of art. In Santayana's day the subject matter would have been called morals. The French still use the word *moralité* in this fashion, though the practice itself seems to be almost as imperiled with them as it is in the United States. The study of morals includes what philosophers currently categorize as "normative ethics." It is best investigated by thinkers who are at home in all the areas of the humanities—in history, literature, and the other arts, as well as in the broadest spectrum of philosophical speculation.

In this realm of the intellect Santayana's contribution is, I believe, superior to the efforts of any other American philosopher. I do not minimize the importance of his work in more technical branches of philosophy—in ontology, epistemology, aesthetics proper—but Santayana's achievement as a humanistic thinker is what I admire most of all.

Concentrating on that aspect of Santayana's productivity, my chapters cluster about his insight into the nature of imagination. In book after book, beginning with *The Sense of Beauty* in 1896 and continuing throughout his career as a philosopher, Santayana charted the ever-present functioning of what he called "the constructive imagination" in human existence.[7] "The systematic relations in time and space," he wrote, "and their dependence upon one another are the work of our imagination. . . . Unless human nature suffers an inconceivable change, the chief intellectual and aesthetic value of our ideas will always come from the creative action of the imagination."[8] The work he did in this area primarily interested the two persons to whom my book is dedicated. From these mentors at Harvard, I first learned how to appreciate Santayana's thought. Their enthusiasm eventuated in my pilgrimage to the man himself, and that propelled me into the explorations embodied in later pages of this book.

When I studied at Harvard shortly after the Second World War, Henry David Aiken was the most dynamic teacher in philosophy there at the time, and virtually the only one whose interests ranged through all the fields of the humanities. He was the resident aesthetician and a former student of David W. Prall and Ralph Barton Perry. Prall had taught courses similar to Santayana's, and Perry had been a disciple of William James. Through this derivation one could feel that Aiken, at his best, exemplified the spirit and many of the ideals of the Golden Age of Harvard philosophy to which Santayana belonged.

As an undergraduate I had the good fortune to meet Walter Jackson Bate and to become one of the students he befriended. His specialty was English literature of the late eighteenth and early nineteenth century, but he saw in Santayana's belletristic style a living proof that philosophy could still express itself in vibrant and graceful writing. For Bate as for Aiken, philosophy remained a humanistic activity rather than a conglomeration of inquiries into logic, linguistics, or the foundations of science. They revered Santayana as one of the last humanists in this sense of the word. Aiken and Bate were both convinced that liberal education attains its greatest sustenance in writing such as his.

Neither Aiken nor Bate found Santayana's beliefs wholly tenable. At different times in his career, Aiken preferred the philosophy of Hume, the pragmatists, English and American logical analysis, and (for a while) Continental existentialism. At an early age, Bate had fallen under the influence of Alfred North Whitehead, whom he knew in the Society of Fellows at Harvard. Whitehead's idealistic organicism plays a substantive role in Bate's work, whereas Santayana's combination of Platonism and materialism does not.

For Bate as for Aiken, Santayana nevertheless served as a model of what could be attained by literary philosophy and philosophical literary criticism. Aiken detailed Santayana's comprehensive importance in an essay entitled "George Santayana: Natural Historian of Symbolic Forms," and Bate chose him as the only twentieth-century philosopher writing in English who was worth including in his anthology of the history of criticism.[9] Whitehead himself, when asked which living philosopher was "most likely to be read in the future," is reported to have answered: Santayana.[10]

When I began to read Santayana, in one of Aiken's courses, books like *Reason in Art, The Sense of Beauty,* and *Interpretations of Poetry and Religion* initially seemed to me somewhat archaic and very unequal in quality. Much of their contents I could not understand, and long stretches appeared precious and overblown. I could see the many evidences of a brilliant mind, but I was not able to perceive the coherent structure that unifies Santayana's statements in even these early works. During a year that I spent at Oxford doing graduate study, I read *The Last Puritan* as an antidote to the philosophy of ordinary language that was practiced there in those days (1949–50). The novel left me unsatisfied, however, and it was almost out of determination to discover what I had been missing that I decided to look for Santayana himself when I would be in Italy the following summer.

I had no idea where he was living, but someone suggested that the authorities at San Giovanni in Laterano—the Mother Church of Rome—would surely know. I went there and talked to a priest who became very indignant when I referred to Santayana as an American philosopher. "He is *not* an American," he said. "He is a Spaniard." I muttered something about Santayana's having lived in America for forty years, but the priest continued to glower and so I turned away. But then an inner voice must have moderated his anger at my obvious ignorance. He called me back and told me that Santayana was living in the sanatorium of the English Blue Nuns adjacent to the Church of Santo Stefano Rotondo.

I was surprised at how easy it was to meet Santayana. Having learned that I was a graduate student at Harvard, he sent word that he would welcome a visit the following afternoon. I hardly knew what to expect. The only great philosopher I had ever met was Alfred North Whitehead. In December 1947, when I was still an undergraduate, Bate had pushed me into a telephone booth and insisted that I call the Whitehead residence. Mrs. Whitehead answered the phone and arranged for me to see her husband immediately. I had an hour's conversation with him two weeks before he died. Dressed in a dark suit and wearing a bright blue cravat, the eighty-year-old Whitehead looked cherubic. Having tea with him was like chatting with a modest and extremely gentle parson who had somehow been transplanted from Cambridge, England, to Cambridge, Massachusetts. He was reluctant to talk about himself or his ideas. He remarked that he no longer read the books and articles on his philosophy that were sent to him—"I just turn the pages occasionally," he said—but he was eager to know what was going on in the world of philosophy in general. He kept asking what the young people at Harvard were interested in nowadays.

My visit with Santayana was totally different. Since it was a hot day in August and my wife and I were bicycling through the countryside, I arrived dressed in scanty Italian shorts. When Santayana opened the door to his room in the sanatorium, his first words were: "I am so glad that you are dressed informally. For I am always, as you see, in my pajamas." For about three hours Santayana regaled us with reflections about everything that came to mind. He seemed to want to talk only about the world as he experienced it, about himself and his ideas. He asked very few questions that might encourage a response to his monologue. I later learned that in this period of his life (he was then eighty-six) Santayana was having difficulties with his hearing. Like many people who are afraid that they will not be able to catch what is being said, he doubtless spoke more continuously than he would have in earlier days. When Gore Vidal paid a visit in 1948, Santayana told him: "I shall talk and you shall listen. . . . You can ask questions, of course. But remember I am *very* deaf."[11]

But possibly that was not the only explanation. Years later Isaiah Berlin told me something relevant that he had heard, in what I assume was the late 1930s, from Mary Berenson, the wife of Bernard Berenson. She mentioned that Santayana had been their houseguest for some time at the Villa I Tatti outside Florence. When Santayana returned to Rome, he wrote her a routine thank-you note. In it he said how much he enjoyed conversing with her husband, whom he knew as a fellow student at Harvard, and he added words to the effect that he had not realized that Bernard was such a good talker. According to Berlin, Mrs. Berenson then exclaimed: "Good talker! How would he know? He wouldn't let anyone else get a word in edgewise. He did all the talking himself and never stopped."

For our part, my wife and I were so thoroughly captivated by Santayana's discourse that we had no desire to interrupt. We felt honored that he was willing to lavish upon us this flow of animated language that issued so effortlessly from him. At his ease in an armchair close to his narrow bed in the small room that he inhabited, he treated us like friends or grandchildren to whom he could speak freely. He learned very little about us to justify his friendliness, but possibly the link to Harvard was sufficient. He showed hardly any curiosity about what was happening there, and the Wittgensteinian philosophy that I had been studying at Oxford intrigued him not at all. He seemed rather scornful of Sartre's kind of existentialism. He referred to Daniel Cory, who was his closest disciple and who later became his literary executor and biographer, as a "half-educated man."

Among the students Santayana had at Harvard, he named only two who were now famous: T. S. Eliot and Walter Lippmann. He was very much concerned about world affairs. The Korean War was at its height, and he was worried about the possibility of an American defeat. He continually used the first person plural in referring to things American—"our forces in Korea," "the war we are in"—and I wondered what the priest would think of his blatant Americanism.

The English that Santayana spoke seemed clearly American in its accent, but with a slight English articulation that sounded very beautiful to me. The Colombian philosopher Mario Laserna recently informed me that when he met Santayana in 1948 they talked in Spanish. I asked Laserna what kind of Spanish accent Santayana had. To which he replied, with some amusement: "An *American* accent!"

At one point I said something about *The Sense of Beauty*. Santayana answered that he wrote the book only because he was coming up for tenure at Harvard and his friends had warned him that in order to keep his job he would have to publish a scholarly work. "But what can I write about?" he had asked them. "There's that course of lectures you've been giving on aesthetics," someone suggested. "Why not that?" Santayana laughed as he added that he followed this advice just to stay on at Harvard. Then he remarked: "But I hadn't *seen* anything." Either at that point or later in the conversation, he leaped up and threw open his casement window in order to show us the view of Rome—although he himself was partly blind.

After a couple of hours had elapsed, a sister entered with Santayana's sparse dinner on a tray. My wife and I quickly rose to leave. Santayana got up too, but talked on for another forty-five minutes. Although his food was getting cold, as we pointed out, he refused to take any notice of it. Standing awkwardly, I allowed my eyes to wander through the room. They lighted on two travel-weary suitcases tucked under a table. Santayana followed my gaze. "I know they're old and battered," he said, "but they've been all over Europe with me." It was as if he felt a need to justify possessing such unsightly articles. His caring about this diminished slightly my admiration. It was fully restored, however, when I mentioned that we hoped to return to Rome in a year or so and would like to see him again. A meager smile appeared on his lips and a look of serene indifference shone in his eyes as he replied, "I may be here."

The following day our friends David Wheeler and his future wife Bronia also visited Santayana. They talked with him about Proust and Kafka, and reported that he listened attentively to their ideas. He said to them, half quizzically, something he had also said to us: "I don't suppose anyone still believes in immortality." When Bronia insisted that she did, Santayana brushed this aside and asserted that the only kind of immortality he could believe in was the eternal and immutable fact that he had lived in time exactly as he had. Nothing else made sense to him. This comports with what he wrote about life and death in *The Realm of Essence:* "Our distinction and glory, as well as our sorrow, will have lain in being something in particular, and in knowing what it is."[12]

I left Santayana with the feeling that he was a lonely man, an old philosopher who would soon be dying by himself in Rome. The brilliance of his conversation was largely lost on me. It was only afterward, when I had studied his major works, that I realized how profound a thinker he was. By then I had forgotten almost everything he had said during our visit. What remained, however, and has been strengthened throughout the passing decades, is my conviction that Santayana was—in Henry James's characterization of what every would-be writer should be—"one of the people on whom nothing is lost."[13]

2   His Host the World

THE FINAL PART of *Persons and Places,* Santayana's autobiography, is entitled *My Host the World.* Like the other two segments, it was originally published as a separate volume. It appeared posthumously, in accordance with Santayana's wishes. Completed ten years before his death, it actually antedates *The Idea of Christ in the Gospels* and *Dominations and Powers.* Santayana's last decade was not an eventful one, however, and could well be omitted from the history of his experiences with persons as well as places. Living in a single room of the sanatorium in Rome, Santayana spent his last years in greater seclusion than before, allowing himself even fewer contacts with persons and even fewer opportunities for direct observation of where and how they lived.

The word *even* is significant here because, as the autobiography shows, Santayana never sought a wide range of involvement with either human beings or their habitations. In a long life, the last forty years of which were blessed with financial and occupational freedom, Santayana knew many individuals and lived in or visited several countries. But the individuals were generally academic acquaintances or school friends or relatives, and in none of the countries did Santayana make much attempt to share the petty but inescapable problems of ordinary people pursuing the everyday activities of political, social, and economic routine. Like Socrates, Santayana was, and wanted to be, a gadfly; but unlike Socrates, he refused to become a gadabout. His place was in the enclosed garden, not the open agora.

Santayana was not possessive: he had no desire to accumulate an enormous wealth of indiscriminate observation and behavior. Like Plato, Pater, Spinoza, and Schopenhauer (a strange assortment no doubt, but all of them greatly influenced him) Santayana cultivated not experience but its efflorescence, not exemplifications of life but its values and recurrent patterns of existence. He wished, above all, to combine the inventiveness of a poet with the integrity of a philosopher. For this kind of occupation he did not need the agora; indeed, the flora and fauna that he would find there might only confuse and arrest.

At the same time, Santayana was neither bigoted nor absolutistic. He knew that his imagination, if not his actual experience, must be stocked, like Noah's ark, with something of each kind. Life was multifarious, and he had no intention, in his re-creation of it, to squeeze everything into one constraining category. He wanted to view the things of this world from the unity of his own personality, and in terms of his own creative interests; but he realized that all things, from their own point of view, had inherent variations that could not be reduced away. "The full-grown human soul should respect all traditions and understand all passions; at the same time it should possess and embody a particular culture, without any unmanly relaxation or mystical neutrality."[1] Out of these two strands the autobiography is woven: the detached sympathy with all persons and places contrasting, sometimes painfully, with the necessity to live as a particular person in a particular place.

As far as Santayana's philosophical ideas are concerned, *Persons and Places* adds little that is new. Instead, it places his philosophy in a vital context and indicates the underlying problems that motivate so much of his thinking. An author's world outlook is as much a function of the questions that he asks of the world as it is of the answers he happens to provide. The answers can be neatly presented in a technical work, such as *Scepticism and Animal Faith* or *Realms of Being;* but the adequate exposition of fundamental questions requires something like *The Last Puritan* or the Platonizing sonnets or the *Soliloquies* or, specifically, this autobiography.

From *Persons and Places* it becomes wholly clear that the problems that were personally most significant to Santayana were the problems neither of action nor of feeling, but rather of belief. Problems of action are concerned with humanity's practical relations within itself and to its environment; they spring from the inescapable need to make moral choices and defensible decisions. Those who, like Hamlet, cannot act in a consecutive and meaningful manner tend to interpret life's problems as a search for purposive behavior and freedom of the will. It is in these terms that most American authors of the nineteenth and early twentieth century saw the world. Writers as different as Henry James and Theodore Dreiser portray men and women who are happy or fulfilled only to the extent that they are able to *do* something, to impose whatever talents and sensitivities they may have upon circumstances that require decisiveness and moral vigor. The mainstream of pragmatism, behaviorism, scientific naturalism, and even their more recent derivatives stems from a similar source.

Problems of feeling originate in a different impulse. They arise from the typically human desire to commune directly with things and people other than oneself. This craving for felt immediacy, for spontaneous understanding and appreciation, for intuition in short, underlies the efforts of writers as disparate as Augustine, on the one hand, and Pascal, Bergson, and Proust on the other.

For Santayana, however, these types of problem were not preeminent. He generally envisaged freedom less as the ability to act than as the ability *not* to act. He did not recognize any supreme achievement in the mere effort to change the world; and he presupposed that the good life depended upon moral resolution—for him there was no burning issue there. Likewise, he took it for granted that one must learn how to cultivate one's feelings adequately and with imagination. From the beginning of the autobiography to the end, one does not get the impression that Santayana's powers of sensitive awareness developed greatly. In his life as a whole they seem to have remained constant: refined and impeccable, no doubt, but static, not dynamic. One does not sense that he had anything like the growth of feeling that is recorded in *The Remembrance of Things Past* or Pascal's *Pensées*.

To say all this is only to indicate that questions about action and feeling were, for Santayana, less pressing than questions about belief. If he had "a white marble mind," as William James remarked, it was true only with respect to the matters that touched him more remotely. For him, the most urgent aspects of life centered about our need to seek the truth and hold fast to it regardless of the consequences to oneself or others. Unlike James, Santayana wanted to articulate beliefs that were warranted not because they worked or served as a personal convenience but simply because, in some ultimate and irreducible manner, they were *true*. Santayana was convinced that the need to act and to feel are secondary to the need to distinguish appearance from reality or sophistry from logic. In many important ways his philosophy closely resembled both pragmatism and intuitionism, but always in the context of a more pervasive scholasticism and rationalism.

Because Santayana sought the truth as something sacrosanct and independent, he insisted upon the skepticism to which his thinking led him. Pragmatism repelled him in that regard. Although its project was based on doubts as extreme as his, he felt that it slurred over this part of philosophy for fear of undermining an opportunism that Santayana considered both facile and futile. He believed that pragmatism was not completely honest: it was too quick in getting people to do something. It was willing to wink complacently over the inveterate limitations of the human situation. Santayana wished to take a long look at the fragility and the pettiness of our species before he came round to the need for active engagement, for ethical and political choice. Intuitionism, on the other hand, lacked the interest in reflection that pragmatism at least retained. Intuitionism besotted itself with faith in unreliable feelings, he thought; it absurdly expected emotion to succeed where thought had failed. Santayana was willing to tolerate Romantic excursions into the unknown, but he denied that they were likely to lead to the truth.

As the basis of his concern about authentic belief and what is true, Santayana distinguished between two elements of the human mind: reason and spirit. The former was part of the animal organism that acts and feels and is located in space and time—the "psyche," as Santayana called it. Reason was responsible for the intelligent adaptation of the psyche to its environment. Reason was practical and could help establish a working harmony with nature. Spirit, however, was an outsider to the purposive necessities of our being. It was both detached and immaterial, a disinterested observer that could as easily sympathize with entities remote in space and time as with those that were near. In fact, it could refuse to serve the needs of the very psyche from which it sprang; and even when it cooperated, it did so only as a spectator, not as an agent.

On Santayana's conception, spirit has the capacity to intuit the essences of things—their defining character or "whatness." This comes to us through the qualitative aspect of experience. But spirit could not hold commerce with the substance of things—their brute presentness, factuality, or "thatness." Spirit was alien to the dynamic workings of a material world in flux. As something nonmaterial, spirit was inevitably doomed, like Cassandra or Tiresias, to see all yet act on nothing. While reason might enable an organism to survive and be happy, spirit could only make it dispassionately aware of what is true, good, and beautiful. Without reason one could not live well; without spirit one could not attain clarity, insight, or fundamental integrity. Without spirit one could not *believe* as one should and regardless of what it costs.

How then is the problem of belief crucial to all of Santayana's thinking? In the last pages of *Persons and Places,* he speaks of "the double conflict, the social opposition and the moral agony, that spirit suffers by being incarnate." Still, he goes on to say, "if it were not incarnate it could not be individual, with a situation in space and time, a language and special perspectives over nature and history: indeed, if not incarnate, spirit could not *exist* at all. . . . [It is] the fate of all spirit to live in a special body and a special age, and yet, for its vocation and proper life, to be addressed from that centre to all life and to all being."[2]

This reveals the radical dilemma that pervaded Santayana's sense of reality. We can believe properly, and as a result act and feel properly, only when spirit is able to wander freely. But spirit cannot exist without the prisonlike shelter of some particular body, some particular set of habits, some particular culture or tradition. How then can spirit ever be free; how can we know with any assurance that we are approximating the truth; how in other words can the "full-grown human soul" understand and correctly respect all other persons or traditions at the same time as it embodies a specific culture of its own?

In his search for an answer to these questions, Santayana begins as a skeptic and ends as a person who understands the importance of what he calls "animal faith." On the one hand, he denies that we can avoid error except by restraining all interpretation of the world as it impinges upon us. One way of living in the spirit would be to strip our consciousness to the sheer apprehension of sensory essences, eliminating the cognitive elements of life that make knowledge possible. We would then encounter reality without actually knowing anything about it, much as an idiot might. On the other hand, skepticism is for Santayana mainly a "heuristic pose"; and he effectively employs it as a midstation on the way to faith in our being as conscious emanations of material nature.

Far from being limited to the vacuous certainty of immediate sensation, the level of spirit that Santayana finally recommends encompasses the plenitude and qualitative richness of experience. It belongs to an individual who lives in the ordinary world and yet manages to go beyond its mundane and moral necessities. To do this is to see things as they are in their essential being, in terms of their uniqueness as well as their historical locus in reality. This is the office of the saint, who exists as an animal organism but achieves contemplative detachment that enables him or her to find the truth and to rise above mere animal interest.

In advocating this kind of saintliness, Santayana did not want to identify his view with that of traditional religion. The churchly saints had too often been ascetics; and all supernatural dogmas that claim to be literal truth Santayana rejected as either superstition or fallacious physics. But though he considered the existence of God dubious in principle, Santayana was not *just* an atheist. From childhood on, he retained a strong attachment to Catholicism as the culture within which he had matured and to which, willy-nilly, he was emotionally attached. He would no sooner renounce Catholicism than he would renounce his parents or the animal side of his nature. But as his parents' views were not his, and as the search for salvation required the subordination of one's animal nature, so too did he refuse to distort his naturalistic beliefs for the sake of the Catholic feelings that he had grown up with.

During the conversation described in the previous chapter, Santayana told my wife and me that upon entering Santo Stefano he had informed the authorities that he was a nonpracticing Catholic. And then he continued: "They sent me priests to try to convert me, and I argued with them. They went away baffled: the old professor knew more about it than they did! But the Mother Superior and some of the nuns are nice, and I let them leave a Bible in my room. Now I'm worried that at the end I may have a protracted illness, or be in a coma for some time, and they'll be standing around waiting for a last-minute conversion. It can be awfully embarrassing."

The struggle between Catholicism and naturalism that disturbed the youthful Santayana, recorded and dramatized in his early sonnets, closely paralleled the conflict between religion and science that troubled many reflective persons of the time. In this respect, as in others, Santayana was a representative product of the nineteenth century. Still, not everyone resolved the conflict in the way that he did. His student T. S. Eliot is an interesting example of one who did not. Like Santayana, Eliot considered the subordination of feelings to beliefs to be the main problem of life; but whereas Santayana's feelings were religious and his beliefs naturalistic, Eliot's feelings were naturalistic or skeptical and his beliefs religious. The main thoroughfare of Eliot's writing is one long consecration to his Christian beliefs, and the documentation of his attempt to subdue whatever sentiments or emotions might distract him from those beliefs. Even about religious feelings, Eliot agreed with T. E. Hulme when Hulme said one ought not to "put up with the dogma for the sake of the sentiment, but . . . possibly swallow the sentiment for the sake of the dogma."[3]

Eliot's leading problem being similar to Santayana's, it would be interesting to know just how the teacher influenced the student. The evidence is unclear. In some matters, Santayana surely had some effect upon Eliot: the latter's doctrine of the "objective correlative," for instance, is a virtual restatement of Santayana's views about "correlative objects" which had appeared in *Interpretations of Poetry and Religion* almost twenty years earlier.[4] In questions about religious faith, Santayana's approach was clearly abhorrent to Eliot. Unlike him and Hulme, Santayana believed that the dogmas of all supernatural religions can be justified only as imaginative portrayals of human aspiration. For him religion is, and of a right ought to be, nothing more than poetry supervening upon life. As a kind of aesthetic metaphysics or mythmaking, religion elicits the most elevated feelings and it provides affective reassurance of a sort that science cannot give. But according to Santayana, religion has no authority to contradict science. In its valid function religion can only depict ideal (and therefore nonexistent) essences. Only science describes the realm of material substance, which includes all existence but nothing that is perfect and much that is quite the opposite. At the same time, religion conveys essences of perfection, which can delight and possibly give us something to live for even though they do not actually exist. It was this duality that William James had in mind when he ambiguously called Santayana's philosophy a "perfection of rottenness."

The transition from orthodox Catholicism to a more or less orthodox naturalism was not without struggle for the young Santayana. He underwent a period of despair and disillusion comparable to the experience of James Joyce's character Stephen Daedalus, who also felt the conflict between naturalistic beliefs and Catholic feelings, and who also refused to subordinate the former to the latter. "I was quite sure," Santayana writes about this stage of his development, "that life was not worth living; for if religion was false everything was worthless, and almost everything, if religion was true. . . . I saw the . . . alternative between Catholicism and complete disillusion; but I was never afraid of disillusion, and I have chosen it."[5]

Together with this disillusionment came a sense of isolation, a feeling of disharmony between his preferences and the demands of the world into which he had been cast by chance. Like many another, Santayana felt the oppression of living in a community that seemed money-mad. The nineteenth century was not only a period in which religion and science parted company, at least temporarily, but also one in which the artist or lover of life felt himself increasingly alienated from the rest of a commercialized society. The result was a desiccated aestheticism and a progressive withdrawal by the artists that allowed society to become even more overtly philistine. As a young man, Santayana was too formalistic and precise to be considered bohemian, but he *was* a poet and he did hold some form of suspicious Platonism and he did flourish a warm and ironic Latinity in the face of cold and moralistic New England. When Santayana was in line for promotion to assistant professor at Harvard, President Charles W. Eliot had his misgivings: "I have doubts and fears about a man so abnormal as Dr. Santayana. The withdrawn, contemplative man who takes no part in the everyday work of the institution, or of the world, seems to me to be a person of very uncertain value. He does not dig ditches, or lay bricks, or write schoolbooks, his product is not of the ordinary useful, though humble, kind. What will it be? It may be something of the highest utility; but, on the other hand, it may be something futile, or even harmful, because unnatural and untimely."[6]

After William James strongly urged the appointment, President Eliot relented. But he was all too right in thinking that for Santayana the practical routine of teaching at Harvard, or anywhere else, was not the *summum bonum*. In his autobiography Santayana refers to this time in his life as "somnambulistic."[7]

But despair and disillusion did not last. They were only the transitional means by which Santayana shook off his conventional "once-born" state in order to return, with greater wisdom, to the task of disintoxicating spirit from the material interests of the organism. Detachment of this sort was not a separation from reality but rather a technique by which spirit could assert its dominance over the feelings and actions of the body to which it was inevitably joined. One renounced the world in order to get it back in greater purity—in particular, the purity of fraternal friendship, untrammeled imagination, and formulated truth. This is what Santayana means when he says that the passion of sublimated love, far from being bloodless, is rather "essentially the spiritual flame of a carnal fire that has turned all its fuel into light."[8]

Human freedom would therefore depend upon the reconciliation of body and soul, psyche and spirit, and not the total renunciation of either. It is true that much of Santayana's later writing was devoted to the description of what sheer spirituality—the life of a wholly independent spirit—could be. But he always insisted that spirituality is only one aspect of human nature, only one of the factors that might contribute to liberation. The mystics sought to eliminate everything other than spirituality, but Santayana by no means implied that their life was the best or only good one, and he never suggested that it was what he desired for himself.

All the same, misinterpretation of Santayana's later work has led many philosophers, notably his pragmatists in America, to infer that Santayana's ethical theory altered massively as he grew older. This is how they describe the change: As a young man, Santayana devoted all of his five-volume book *The Life of Reason* to the thesis that the good life can be attained only through the harmonization of the various impulses that naturally conflict within the human animal. A decision would be morally sound if it helped to integrate all or most of one's interests, and harmonization of this sort required employment of practical reason. In other words, Santayana's earlier ethical theory is presumed to have invoked a standard of intelligence for the determination of what counts as an "objectively moral act," which is to say, an act that can justifiably be recommended for all persons similarly situated. On the other hand, his later theory is thought to have renounced the ideal of intelligence for one that advocates an interest in contemplated essences, an interest that is accepted and approved not because it harmonizes best with other interests but merely because it is the interest of spirituality. As logicians, Santayana's critics complained that he often contradicted himself since he failed to recognize the shift in his thinking; and as moralists, they found his second ethical standard distinctly inferior to his first one.

I find this argument unconvincing. Santayana's later writings do not include a fundamental variation in theory, though they do indicate a "change of climate," as he puts it. However confusing his language may have been, Santayana never treated either rationality or spirituality as an ultimate and objective standard. He called himself a "moral relativist," by which he meant, among other things, that neither the life of reason nor the life of spirit can justifiably be recommended for all persons under all circumstances. His earlier defense of the life of reason, and his eventual focus on the contemplation of essences, should therefore be taken more as expressions of his own predilections than as theoretical or doctrinal positions in ethics.

As a young man, Santayana sided with the rational world and judged spirituality, like everything else, in terms of its results. His judgment was caustic, as may be seen from his repudiation of mysticism. Also, he was confident that most worldly impulses could be harmonized and a stable political order imposed upon them. As an older man, Santayana shed that illusion. He came to realize that a life of reason was a precarious attainment, its victories being slight and often doubtful. His renewed interest in spirit, as an indispensable part of human nature, deepened his sympathy with the contemplative life and even mysticism. He could now imagine the condition of one who stood against the world and chose renunciation rather than harmonization. He learned to appreciate the message of the Indians as well as that of the Greeks, although he himself still preferred the latter. In *The Realm of Essence* he asserts: "I frankly cleave to the Greeks and not to the Indians, and I aspire to be a rational animal rather than a pure spirit."[9]

We may say, then, that Santayana more or less retained his preference for the life of reason. But he never suggested that his preferences, whatever they might be, were to serve as the bases of an objective moral code. When he defends the life of reason, as a young man, or takes the part of someone who aspires to be a pure spirit, in his later years, he is only presenting the implications of a possible way of life. He does not tell his readers which one they ought to follow, and at times he specifically denies that *ought* can be used in that fashion at all.

Still, this does not prevent Santayana from believing in objective standards on another and more crucial level. He says that we ought to take our stand, whether it be with the rational world or against it, in the light of what we are, as distinct from what we think we are. Concerning the antagonism between a master-passion (which spirituality, the renunciation of all passion, may itself paradoxically become) and the dedication to harmony or reason, he states: "The ethics of this conflict are the same as in other conflicts: to know oneself, and to impose on oneself or on others only the sacrifices requisite to bring one's chosen life to perfection."[10]

In the final analysis, it would appear that Santayana does believe in an objective standard of ethical value and that he is not, to this extent, a moral relativist. He ordains that our preferences are justifiable only when they emanate from knowledge of what we really are and what we really want. And this, in its own dimension, virtually reinstates the ideal of a life of reason; for, as Santayana believes, we cannot have knowledge without rationality. Consequently, I would further disagree with those critics who claim that Santayana's later philosophy relinquishes the objective standard of intelligence. In the only sense in which he consistently held that standard as a young man, he also did at the end of his career. Like the pragmatists, he was, both early and late, a relativist insofar as he denied that one could determine, in advance, which way of life is best for anyone. But he accepted intelligence as an objective and moral standard inasmuch as he held that valid decisions could not be made without reasoned insight into a person's nature. Santayana maintained, as did the pragmatists, that the good life for human beings is whatever life that rationally harmonizes their various interests and passions in accordance with the "real nature" in each of them as individuals.

But how are we to know what someone's "real nature" is? Santayana does not tell us. To this degree his philosophy is surely insufficient for the needs of practical decision making. He simply expects people to settle the matter for themselves; and that, as he admits, avoids the issue instead of solving it. Nevertheless, in *The Last Puritan* Santayana gives us something that may be better than a decision procedure for determining what one's nature is. Within its fictional parameters his novel presents a detailed portrait of two young men, each of whom gains insight into what he truly is, though only one can live successfully in conformance with this realization.

Oliver Alden, "the last puritan," strives for spiritual emancipation without learning, until it is too late, that he is doing so. His development is warped and frustrated by his puritanical surroundings and by the fact that the world is never hospitable to those who seek perfection. Like Santayana himself, Oliver is troubled by the problem of belief, not of action or feeling. Until the end he retains his rigorous and puritanical ability to act, and the need to refine his feelings was not a driving force in his experience. What mattered most for Oliver was the discovery of some concept or ideal *worth* acting for, a plan of life that his intellect could accept as veridical in view of what reality is. He has a passionate hunger for the truth, and he finally receives his crowning epiphany when he perceives that he has deluded himself in his relations to the men and women he thought he loved: "I was not seeing the reality in them at all, but only an image, only a mirage, of my own aspiration."[11]

In the prologue Santayana sums up Oliver's "secret" as something "common enough, if you like, and even universal, since it was simply the tragedy of the spirit when it's not content to understand but wishes to govern" (16–17). If only Oliver had been content to understand, he might have seen the reality both in his friends and in the world. As it is, he fails to reach salvation or completion because he cannot solve the problem of belief. On puritan grounds he concludes that it is wrong to be a puritan, but he never thinks his way through to a defensible alternative.

If Oliver represents lonely and pathetic spirit doomed to misery in a world devoted to action or feeling, Mario Van de Weyer, his cousin, embodies the harmony between natural impulses and the jubilant life of reason. Mario, who does not worry about the meaning of life, is able to think, act, and feel in a manner that is adequate for his happiness. He just naturally succeeds in everything he undertakes. He is cultivated, witty, shrewd, considerate, and even kind, but he has little of the spirituality that characterizes Oliver, and none of his puritanism. Mario is as Latin as Oliver is Nordic, as Catholic as Oliver is Protestant. His is a sunny daylight, not the dark night of the soul. Unlike Oliver, he fulfills his true nature.

In painting these two contrasting portraits, Santayana is not merely personifying the life of spirit and the life of reason. He is also, as he indicates in the preface, portraying different vectors within his own nature, different tensions that had to be reconciled in order for him, or anyone like him, to lead a good life. By means of narrative depiction, if not by argument or analysis, he is pointing to that element of idiosyncratic personality with which all moral deliberation must concern itself. He is revealing what *his* real nature is, and how it had to struggle with the circumvening world in order to achieve integrity.

What Santayana means by "real nature" may also be seen from his conception of the self. At this point the ethics and politics of the pragmatists do part company with Santayana's. From the differences between Santayana and the pragmatists about the nature of the self, together with the fact that Santayana subordinates problems of action, spring all their mutual distrust, mistaken criticism, and inability to appreciate one another.

The two conceptions of the self can be illustrated as follows:

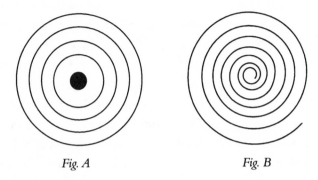

Fig. A   Fig. B

Figure A represents the self as a core or kernel with concentric circles around it. The circles are the experiences of the self, none of which touch it but all of which enclose it and hide it from the outside. Figure B represents the self as a spiral whose structure, contours, and direction themselves include interaction with the environment. As a result, there is nothing in the spiral to allow any viable distinction between the self and its experience.

According to the kernel theory of personality, the self is "really" separate from its experience. The events that impinge upon a person change him only in the sense of adding new attributes to his character and making him seem different. The kernel of his being never changes, and it is with this that his real nature is to be identified. Although this core may be hard to discover or define, it amounts to what the individual is "in his heart"; all the incrustations of his overt development are outer layers that can in principle be stripped away.

On the kernel theory one's involvement with other persons, things, or ideals can only be such as to draw out what one really is anyhow. In an unhappy life, the outer layers are opaque to the kernel; they smother and distort it. When life is gratifying, however, the kernel controls and profits from the concentric circles of experience. To secure salvation one must recognize one's own kernel and live according to its unique attributes. Other persons, however intimate, can never know the kernel of one's being; and it is this that leads Pascal, for instance, to despair of merely human love: "What is the Ego? . . . Does he who loves someone on account of beauty really love that person? No; for the small-pox, which will kill beauty without killing the person, will cause him to love her no more. And if one loves me for my judgment, memory, he does not love *me,* for I can lose these qualities without losing myself. Where, then, is this Ego, if it be neither in the body nor in the soul? And how love the body or the soul, except for these qualities which do not constitute *me,* since they are perishable?"[12]

The spiral theory denies that there is any inner kernel to be identified with one's real nature. At any moment a person is just the sum total of his or her experiences. They constitute the spiral as it exists at a particular point and then leads on to further convolutions. On this view there is no break between the self and its experience, for experience *is* the self: in toto, the self is only a series of past, present, and future experiences. By phrases like "real nature" or "true self" the spiral theory refers to nothing but the ongoing or self-sustaining condition of an organism. In order to know whether someone is fulfilling his or her real nature, we would look not for integrity with an underlying core of personhood, but rather for a spiral that harmoniously wends its way through the universe. Madame Merle, in Henry James's *The Portrait of a Lady,* presents this idea as follows: "There's no such thing as an isolated man or woman; we're each of us made up of some cluster of appurtenances. What shall we call our 'self'? Where does it begin? Where does it end? It overflows into everything that belongs to us—and then it flows back again. I know a large part of myself is in the clothes I choose to wear. I've a great respect for *things!* One's self—for other people—is one's expression of one's self; and one's house, one's furniture, one's garments, the books one reads, the company one keeps—these things are all expressive."[13]

Neither Santayana nor pragmatists like John Dewey and William James consistently hold to either of these theories of human personality. But while the pragmatists strongly emphasize the spiral theory, Santayana leans most heavily on the kernel theory. At the hard inner core he would not place the entire self but only an individual spirit. The outer layers that wrap spirit around are related to the behavior of an organism that cannot survive without purposive action. Although at times the pragmatists seem to recognize something like what Santayana calls spirit, their entire orientation refuses to dissociate mind from practical necessities. As a result, their thinking easily merges with behavioristic philosophies, and even when they are not limiting themselves to motor action, they tend to interpret consciousness as itself dynamically active in an indirect, if not explicit, fashion. For the most part, pragmatism denies that anything like spirit can be distinguished from the more or less intelligent conduct of an organism that exists through interaction with its environment. The self is therefore contingent upon its social and biological development and cannot harbor any private or inviolable core.

In his opposition to pragmatism, Santayana admits that spirit comes into being only as the offshoot of material processes, but he insists that it is inherently different from any of them. He believes there is in human consciousness a *something* that observes our dependence upon the environment without itself being constituted by that circumstance. Unlike Pascal, Santayana does not think the kernel is immortal or supremely valuable in its purified isolation; but like Pascal, he asserts that this mental entity must not be confused with the experience that encircles it. In the autobiography we often find him making statements such as these: "I might wish to change my surroundings and my way of living; I never undertook to change myself. I regard my occupations and interests somewhat as an actor regards his various parts or a painter his subjects."[14]

Santayana's allegiance to some form of the kernel theory serves to clarify many of his other attitudes toward life, as well as the basis of his quarrels with pragmatism. For instance, it is not surprising that, despite his love of order and tradition, Santayana's political views were essentially those of nineteenth-century liberalism, just as it is not surprising that Dewey's politics were basically collectivistic. If there is no kernel and our personalities are wholly dependent upon interaction with the environment, the self can never really be detached from either nature or society. As a result, collectivism becomes the groundwork upon which individual liberties must be conceived and constructed.

If, however, we start from Santayana's point of departure, as did Locke and the American founding fathers, we think of people as separate kernels that the state ought not to tamper with. Society and nature alike may be useful, even indispensable, for the happiness of the kernel, but they can have only derivative importance. They are mere instrumentalities. On the pragmatic view, we are primordially a part of each other, so that our spirals interweave and we acquire our freedom through the personal stamp that each of us impresses upon the inescapable unity. On Santayana's view, we are residually separate beings whose outer layers overlap without our inner cores ever interpenetrating. And even overlapping, he would say, cannot be justified unless it permits a kernel to reach fulfillment in itself.

Similarly, Santayana's aloofness from political and social duties, and in general his avoidance of communal activities, is explained, or at least symbolized, by his adherence to the kernel theory. It may also account for his tolerant attitude toward the lives that others choose, and his more or less egoistic concern about his own. A person who is secure within his or her kernel need not feel threatened if different people experience the world differently. That only means that their kernels are not the same as our kernel. And neither is ours necessarily in conflict with theirs, or inherently preferable to them. Likewise, one can help other people fulfill themselves not by directly contributing to their welfare, as the spiral theory would suggest, but merely by refusing to impose restrictive outer layers. Because no one can change the inner core, we do best to leave it alone. This, in turn, increases the likelihood of being let alone oneself.

In this context Santayana goes so far as to admit that he is both selfish and heartless in his attempt to "resist human contagion, except provisionally, on the surface, and in matters indifferent to me."[15] Still, as he also points out, his selfishness was never competitive or aggressive. It was instead the self-absorption of a man who tried to live in the spirit at the same time as he remained at home within the life of reason. Did he enjoy the best of both worlds, or did he exclude himself from each in turn? Opinion has varied; and I, for one, would hesitate to judge. Perhaps it is enough to recognize that Santayana's "selfishness" was the devotion of a gardener cultivating what nature gave him. And surely, if the world is not to waste, *some* of its gardeners must live in the way that Santayana did.

This view of Santayana as both a person and a thinker is reinforced by the picture of him that Daniel Cory paints in his memoir *Santayana, the Later Years*.[16] Despite the title, the book is not a life study. It is just an account of the Santayana that Cory knew between the years 1927, when they met, and 1952, when Santayana died. It does, however, amplify what Santayana wrote about himself, and about the world in which he lived. It reveals elements of his personality that fail to emerge from the autobiography. As such, it is vivid and insightful throughout, in places sad and moving. This is so because Cory had the piety or wisdom to let Santayana speak for himself, both in letters and conversations. The letters alone, written to Cory over the period of twenty-five years and sewn together with a slight biographical thread, make up 60 or 70 percent of the contents. In effect, this was one of Santayana's last books.

At their meeting in 1927, Santayana was sixty-three, Cory twenty-two. Long since retired from teaching, Santayana was living in a hotel in Rome, financially secure, peacefully harnessed to a routine of work and leisure, steadily producing the major works of his final years. From this splendid elevation in his life, Santayana was able to write Cory letters that are frank, intimate, freely revealing, and more authentic than many other pages for which Santayana is known.

In the security of his relationship with Cory, Santayana appears more likable than in the collection of letters to other people that Cory edited in a separate volume. There one often senses strain and affectation, as Santayana forces himself to acknowledge a gesture from some remote acquaintance, or tries to justify his existence before those who still count as authorities for him, or else rejects the arguments of an alien critic. Here, however, Santayana speaks his heart openly, boldly, with the simplicity that a great and lonely man might have in addressing a dedicated admirer of his writings.

Even *Persons and Places* lacks the immediacy of a real human being which imbues these letters to Cory. In his autobiography, as in so much of his work, Santayana often reveals his mind and hides his real self. The persons and places that he had encountered are idealized in the autobiography, not in the sense that their impurities are denied but rather in being raised to a level of literary and philosophical dignity, serving as a subject for reflection and the basis of wise generalizations. In this book, Santayana half-consciously, as if he knew what he was doing but preferred not to discuss it, allows himself to pose in his pajamas.

As I have been suggesting, Santayana was not a detached spirit trying to live as a human being. This is evident in his relationship with Cory. To his only protégé, Santayana was willing to appear as something very different: an old man bored by discussions with technical philosophers, flattered by visits from poets better than himself, reading everything that can help him with his own projects, struggling with the vicissitudes of exile, illness, war, and financial fluctuation.

As a narrative of Santayana's later life, the book is mainly a portrait of an author at work. But the letters also reflect the character of the times, and their effect upon Santayana as a human being. One does not sense that the social background of these years changed his thinking very much. By the time Cory met him, his mature philosophy had already coalesced and just needed to be written out. What was not certain, however, was whether Santayana, or anyone else, could escape the hazards of the age long enough to write his kind of philosophy. Even among philosophers, he was, as he says, "a back number, partly in age, partly in manner": "Philosophers now are expected to be thoroughly confused in general, and very scholastic in detail."[17] But the next sentence begins "This doesn't matter"; and he returns to his labors, writing every morning, staying in Italy when Switzerland will not admit him just before the outbreak of war, entering the sanatorium and living in greater solitude than before.

In the course of the narrative, Santayana frequently shows himself as a craftsman reacting to his own writings. Reading over *The Life of Reason* after thirty years, he honestly notes that "the style is, often, verbose and academic, satisfied with stock concepts"; when he sees an old article of his that has been reprinted in a volume on John Dewey, he admits to feeling "a little ashamed . . . not because

I don't think it good enough in itself, but because it is explicitly a translation of Dewey into my own categories, which naturally don't fit"; learning that *The Last Puritan* has been translated into German *aus dem Amerikanischen,* he laments: "Ah! My beautiful Received English wasted!"; when a reviewer calls something of his "boring and obese," he remarks: "What would the critic say if he saw me in the flesh?"[18]

Some of these letters rank with Santayana's best writing. Paragraphs that discuss his current study of Russell, Toynbee, and many others form tiny essays crying to be spoken aloud. In answer to Cory's criticism, there are several pages of a more theoretical sort, dealing with questions about the nature of essence, charity, intent as opposed to intuition, and so on. There are also occasional comments about himself that illuminate large portions of Santayana's later work. When he is told that Russell observed that in his final period Whitehead "yearned for unity," Santayana replies: "What I have all my life yearned for is not unity, but completion."[19] This stands in juxtaposition to passages in *Realms of Being* in which he argues that "the union sought by a liberated spirit is no fusion of its substance with any other substance, but a moral unanimity or fellowship with the life of all substances insofar as they support or enlarge its own life."[20]

Eventually, Cory sees Santayana to the grave. Discussing the nature of death with him, Cory suggests something about "the peace that passeth all understanding." "If it passeth all understanding," Santayana replies, "it's simply nothing. I have no faith, nor find any comfort, in trying to imagine a blind cosmic feeling of peace. . . . I prefer to be frankly poetical and say I am content to rest in the bosom of Abraham."[21] At the end, Cory asks him whether he is in pain, and Santayana feebly utters his last words: "Yes, my friend. But my anguish is entirely physical; there are no moral difficulties whatsoever."[22]

An acquaintance of Santayana's once told me that the only reason he undertook *Persons and Places* was to keep Cory from writing his biography. But Cory has done him no disservice. We can feel glad that Santayana entrusted him with so much choice material that he must have known Cory would make available to whatever world remained hospitable to it.

3   The Last Puritan

WITHIN THE GREAT variety of his achievements as an author and a thinker, Santayana's ability to combine philosophy and literary awareness is paramount in *The Last Puritan*. Throughout the novel the two approaches are organically interrelated. In their unity they reflect his reality as he experienced it. In a letter he wrote in 1921, fourteen years before he finished *The Last Puritan*, Santayana says that his book will "contain all I know about America, about women, and about young men. As this last is rather my strong point,

I have *two* heroes, the Puritan and another not too much the other way. To make up, I have no heroine, but a worldly grandmother, a mother—the quintessence of all New England virtues—and various fashionable, High Church, emancipated, European, and sentimental young ladies. I have also a German governess—in love with the hero—of whom I am very proud."[1]

The Last Puritan, Santayana's only novel, was an immediate bestseller when it appeared in 1935. Two years later Santayana added a preface. In it he discusses the development of the project over a period of forty-five years, as well as his philosophical intentions in this work of fiction. The forty-five-year span that Santayana mentions begins with the period of 1891–93, which Santayana describes in one of his letters as a "second youth of mine [that] was far pleasanter than my first youth."[2] In 1891 Santayana was a philosophy instructor, twenty-seven years old, living as a proctor in Stoughton Hall in Harvard Yard and spending most of his free time in the company of undergraduates at the Delphic Club. That club was "absolutely my home," he reports, adding that his novel originated as a story that had its setting there. During the twenty years that followed, Santayana may have allowed the book to gestate, but he did little writing on it. Only after he resigned from Harvard and gave up residence in the United States did he find that he could proceed. Beginning with the outbreak of World War I, he lived for five years in England, mainly in Oxford, and that renewed association with academia marks the start of consecutive writing of *The Last Puritan.*

Santayana's novel is not a story about university life or under-graduate adventures. Though the principal characters—Oliver and Mario—are still in their twenties at the end of the narrative, and though the plot centers about their progress into manhood, the narrative expresses views that reached fruition during the years of Santayana's own philosophical maturity. By 1935 he was more than halfway through *Realms of Being,* completing final drafts of *The Realm of Truth* and doing preliminary writing for *The Realm of Spirit.* Works such as *Platonism and the Spiritual Life* had been published in the previous decade. *The Last Puritan* embodies the thinking of a seasoned philosopher, seventy-two years old at the time of its publication, whose ideas were largely formulated even though they had not all been written out. As a work of art, the novel derives its underlying form from the dialectical play between the youthful experience of its two main characters and the accomplished vision of the commentator who interprets it for us.

There are, of course, characters in the book who are much older than Oliver and Mario, but their greater age is never presented as giving them access to the philosophic scope that Santayana had himself achieved by the time the novel was finally written. Even Mr. Darnley, the vicar who understands the concepts of spirit that Santayana was later to present in *The Idea of Christ in the Gospels,* hardly approximates Santayana's general insight. It appears in *The Last Puritan* as the framework and designing principle of everything that happens to the characters, everything they do or say, and everything that is said about them.

In 1959, seven years after Santayana died, Corliss Lamont published a *Dialogue on Santayana* to which several philosophers who knew Santayana personally contributed. In the midst of his reminiscences, Horace M. Kallen remarks that the "true image" of Santayana is in *The Last Puritan* rather than *Persons and Places,* which Kallen calls "a shield and a deception really."[3] Later Kallen adds that the novel is "far more authentic than the autobiographical books. Partly because he assumes that it's disguised."[4] If we think of a disguise as a masquerade that does not hide the truth but rather manifests it in

ways that are only available to make-believe, Kallen's suggestion
may be valuable and is worth pursuing.

In doing so, we are immediately arrested by the subtitle of *The
Last Puritan—A Memoir in the Form of a Novel*. A memoir may be
biographical, but it need not be autobiographical. It is an account
based on memory even if it is not one's own existence that is being
remembered. To think of the book as a fictionalized version of
Persons and Places—which portrays the details of Santayana's life—
would seem to be wholly egregious except for the fact that Santayana's experience reveals itself so fully in this memoir of events
that never happened literally to him (or anyone else).

Santayana prepares us for the nature of his masquerade by using
as his epigraph a quotation from the French philosopher who wrote
under the name of Alain. It translates as follows: "It is well said that
experience speaks through the mouth of older men: but the best
experience that they can bring to us is that of their salvaged youth."
The last adjective in this quote is *sauvée,* suggesting that the best that
age can communicate is the part of youth which can be rescued
despite the passage of time. Although he gives himself only a minor role on the peripheries of his novel, Santayana regains his earlier experience in the way that Proust does. Each of them writes his
research into past time from the point of view of one who has long
since outlived it but now seeks, through re-creative imagination,
greater understanding of its inherent meaning than he could have
had when he was actually young himself.

As in the case of Proust's masterpiece, critics and ordinary readers alike have wondered how this memorial novel should be clas-
sified. It often resembles Santayana's essayistic writing, so much so
that Santayana felt a need to justify his making all the characters
sound the way he wrote. In the epilogue Mario complains that
"you make us all talk in your own philosophical style, and not in
the least as we actually jabber" (570). Santayana responds to this

kind of criticism in the preface, and in the epilogue he insists that, far from writing "a philological document," he was creating a work that would remain understandable to future readers who might not be acquainted with the idioms of a single epoch. "Fiction is poetry, poetry is inspiration, and every word should come from the poet's heart, not out of the mouths of other people. . . . Even in the simplest of us passion and temperament have a rich potential rhetoric that never finds utterance; and all the resources of a poet's language are requisite to convey not what his personages would have been likely to say, but what they were really feeling" (570– 71).

   This statement should be read in the context of what Santayana remarks about "literary psychology" in *Scepticism and Animal Faith*. He argues there that no attempt to understand the experience of other people (or ourselves as we existed in the past) can ever have the kind of credibility that science has. What he calls "scientific psychology" seeks objective knowledge by making inferences about the realm of matter out of which experience emerges. To the extent that we think or write about experience in itself—experience as it appears to whoever is having it—we are dealing with immediate qualities, "essences," that cannot be conveyed in any literal or verifiable fashion. To discourse about essences is to engage in literary psychology, which is fictional and poetic—in an extended sense of these words—regardless of how prosaic our language may be. According to Santayana, a writer cannot succeed in expressing what real or imagined people feel by copying their speech patterns, as a linguist might, or by using any other quasi-scientific device. Instead, he must rely upon intuition that typically belongs to art.

   The nature of artistic awareness had earlier been analyzed by Santayana in *The Sense of Beauty*. In all works of art he detected a capacity for expressiveness that goes beyond either material or formal properties in the aesthetic object. Santayana suggests that art attains its appropriate truthfulness to life through a special kind of idealization. Through ordinary idealization human beings conceive of persons or events in an abstract and simplified manner that the imagination presents as beautiful in some degree. If this happens through the elimination of individual differences, the characters turn into types and lose their capacity to represent the quality of human experience. In great works of art, however, that does not happen. For there the artist offers to the imagination of his audience something that is "more striking and living than any reality, or any abstraction from realities."[5] Far from being desiccated types, the great characters in fiction give one an idealized sense of individuality that often seems more natural to us than what is found in nature itself. In a passage that foreshadows what he was later to attempt in *The Last Puritan,* Santayana states:

> A Hamlet, a Don Quixote, an Achilles—[these] are no averages, they are not even a collection of salient traits common to certain classes of men. They seem to be persons; that is, their actions and words seem to spring from the inward nature of an individual soul. Goethe is reported to have said that he conceived the character of his Gretchen entirely without observation of originals. And, indeed, he would probably not have found any. His creation rather is the original to which we may occasionally think we see some likeness in real maidens. It is the fiction here that is the standard of naturalness. . . . Perhaps no actual maid ever spoke and acted so naturally as this imaginary one.[6]

In this context Santayana draws upon Aristotle's dictum about poetry being truer than history. But he also goes beyond Aristotle. The latter thought that history is less "philosophical" than poetry because history tells us about particular occurrences whereas poetry achieves a more universal reference by indicating what some type of person might have said or done on one or another occasion. This alone would not prove that poetry expresses the truth about human individuality; indeed, it could even be taken to mean that poetry differs from history by giving general information.

Santayana rejects any such interpretation. As we saw, he insists that great characters in fiction manifest "the inward nature of an individual soul." In the case of *The Last Puritan,* he thought that duplication of local idioms or dialects would interfere with the proper employment of aesthetic intuition. In order to show what the characters felt, and what they are as human beings, one had to use an imaginative approach that probes more deeply into the philosophical ramifications of their human particularity. That requires the language of someone who can analyze the characters' condition philosophically while also integrating such analysis with the kind of inventiveness needed for the creation of a work of art.

In developing this mode of presentation, Santayana successfully challenges many of our preconceptions about the "realistic" novel. Some people have thought that realism involves a search for quasi-photographic reproduction; and others have claimed that fidelity to "the stream of consciousness" uniquely demonstrates the nature of human experience. In James Joyce's *Ulysses,* both of these techniques are used to good effect. But do they bring us any closer to "the real world" than Santayana's meditative prose? I do not think so. Once the contents of lived experience are rendered into words, they have already become figments of the novelist's mentality. Joyce's figments are no more reliable than Santayana's; they merely reflect a different way of perceiving and digesting reality. The great virtue in Santayana's method consists in its exploration of moral and pervasive problems that people, at least of the sort that he depicts, face throughout their existence—whether or not they can discuss such problems as brilliantly as Santayana and his characters do.

❋

These considerations apply not only to the language that the various personages use or to the soliloquies through which they voice their introspective attitudes, but also to their individuality within the fiction. In the preface Santayana reports that his fable mixes historical and imaginary elements. In letters to friends he states that all the characters are an amalgamation drawn from various people he had known in earlier life. This is the usual procedure in the writing of novels. The models for Santayana's protagonist were several poets in the 1880s and 1890s who seemed to him representative of many intellectuals in America at the time. Though Oliver Alden is unique and wholly imaginary, his story expresses the hopeless plight of other young men whose aspirations found no sustenance in their society. In one place, Santayana says that "all those friends of mine . . . were visibly killed by the lack of air to breathe. People individually were kind and appreciative to them, as they were to me; but the system was deadly, and they hadn't any alternative tradition (as I had) to fall back upon: and . . . they hadn't the strength of a great intellectual hero who can stand alone."[7]

This much of Santayana's theme is hardly unique to him. It is central in *Roderick Hudson,* the early novel of Henry James, and it recurs as a leitmotif through many of James's later works. Like these Jamesian novels, *The Last Puritan* makes no effort to be sociological. The system that Santayana thought so deadly to his friends was the general atmosphere of American life during those decades of industrial expansion and cultural change. But Santayana gives us only meager glimpses into the social realities of New England or even Harvard. As John Dewey observed in the brief review he

wrote soon after the novel appeared, the book includes "extraordi-
narily little background of scene. . . . The scene is scenery; stage setting for the persons who are its characters."[8] To some extent, the
characters were chosen as indications of what was happening in
America at the time, but we do not see them living or acting as
members of a class or major segment of American society. What
kind of system, we may therefore ask, is "the system" to which San-.
tayana refers?

For the most part, it was a system of religious and moral ideas related to what Santayana calls "the genteel tradition." Throughout
the latter half of the nineteenth century, New England attitudes
were dominated by attempts to reconcile Protestantism with the
romanticism that issued out of German idealist philosophy. Emerson, who was a Christian moralist as well as a poet, had given an
example of how this reconciliation might occur. He sought to harmonize a love of nature with a sense of transcendental realities; and
he believed that despite the pantheistic elements in this religious
outlook it remained faithful to the original teachings of Christianity.
When Oliver Alden reaches Harvard in Santayana's novel, he takes
up residence in Emerson's former rooms in Divinity Hall. For Oliver,
as for the young poets whose history he enacts, the Emersonian influence represents much of the setting for his inner struggle.

In his autobiographical writings, Santayana frequently records
his sense of alienation from the Protestant culture of New England.
But one has to remember that he was also a part of it. Though his
parents were Catholic, he grew up within the Protestant milieu to
which his mother was allied through her first marriage. Most of
Santayana's childhood friends were Protestants, and the manners he
acquired in school were those of a proper Bostonian. When I met
him in 1950, his accent seemed to me as close as one could get to
the way that most Boston Brahmins must have sounded in the nineteenth century.

In saying that the prevailing system of American thought had killed the promising young poets and intellectuals, Santayana does not mean that poetry or art or culture in general was scorned by American society. He means that New England, and the country as a whole, failed to recognize that creativity in these areas could be as worthy and morally justifiable as action devoted to more pragmatic ends. The works of art that Americans were accumulating with their newly acquired wealth were usually the product of Europeans and Asians, an offshoot of Mediterranean and Eastern societies whose ethical presuppositions were suspect even though they could somehow provide superior access to beauty. In the United States, as Santayana knew it, there was little place for aesthetic or spiritual creativity: "If a man is born a poet or a mystic in America he simply starves, because what social life offers and presses upon him is offensive to him, and there is nothing else."[9]

The "alternative tradition" upon which Santayana could fall back consisted primarily of the Catholic orientation to which he was introduced as a child. By the time he was eighteen, his belief in Catholic dogma had largely disappeared, and the atheism he openly professed in later life was well-developed in him at some point during the next ten years. What remained, as a constant from beginning to end, was appreciation of the myths and rituals of Catholicism that could embellish everyday experience by making it orderly, ornate, and meaningful. Moreover, he cherished Catholicism as the living residue of Greek and Latin civilization that had survived in the modern world despite the inroads of Nordic and Romantic barbarism.

Emanating from this personal background, Santayana's novel belongs to the genre of accounts by a survivor who tells us about some peril that befell his tribe, and from which only he escaped. There but for the grace of God go I, the survivor says, because he is aware of his identity with those who were not as lucky. At the same time, he lives to tell the tale because of attributes in himself that enabled him to get away, attributes that then become essential ingredients in his narrative. Drawing upon the two traditions in his own experience, Santayana puts them in dramatic opposition to each other as a way of showing why and how his friends were destroyed. In the process, he also demonstrates that he himself survived by creatively harmonizing these opposing ways of life. The young poets who were victims of their society suffered a tragic fate because they were unable to make that kind of integration.

In various places throughout the novel, Santayana emphasizes that Oliver's history is not only sad but also "tragic." The book has elements of comedy, to which I will return, but it is clearly intended to be read as a tragedy. In the German edition, the subtitle becomes: *Die Geschichte eines tragischen Lebens* (the story of a tragic life). Although this eliminates the idea of a memoir in the form of a novel, it is faithful to the contents of the book. Santayana depicts the tragedy of puritanism as it appears in his twentieth-century hero. The puritanism that Oliver Alden embodies is, however, significantly different from the puritanism of his ancestors in the seventeenth century. He is a descendent of the colonial Alden in Longfellow's poem "The Courtship of Miles Standish," and his first name derives from the puritanical Cromwell who overthrew Charles I. But Santayana's protagonist consistently rejects most of the doctrines his predecessors considered fundamental.

For this reason, Ralph Barton Perry's description of *The Last Puritan* is misleading—at least, as far as Oliver is concerned. In *Puritanism and Democracy* Perry says: "Santayana's famous book is an account not of the living puritan creed, but of its death; and its death resembles the death of any creed when its subordinations have become negations, its convictions rigidities, and its surviving zealots monstrosities."[10] Oliver Alden is neither a zealot nor a monstrosity. Santayana portrays him as a superior individual, a very good man, a pilgrim hungering for salvation that eludes him throughout life.

Perry's comment is accurate about Oliver's bluenose uncle, Nathaniel, who appears at the beginning of the novel as a satiric vignette of puritanism as it had degenerated in Victorian Boston. At the end, having failed in his attempt to find love or even contentment in the midst of World War I, Oliver partly reverts to Nathaniel. But even then, Oliver searches for a wholesome and sane puritanism that would be suitable for the present and so remain a living rather than a dead creed. He has long since outgrown the Calvinism of his forebears. Like Irma (his German governess) he believes in the great goodness of nature, and his religious faith—to the degree that he has any—is closer to Goethe's pagan naturalism than to ordinary Christianity.

In calling Oliver the *last* puritan, Santayana did not wish to imply that there will be no others. He originally thought of entitling his book *The Ultimate Puritan;* and in the epilogue he remarks: "A moral nature burdened and over-strung, and a critical faculty fearless but helplessly subjective—isn't that the true tragedy of your ultimate Puritan?" (571–72). In the prologue the character Mario had already told us that "in Oliver puritanism worked itself out to its logical end. He convinced himself, on puritan grounds, that it was wrong to be a puritan. . . . That was the tragedy of it. Thought it his clear duty to give puritanism up, but couldn't" (14).

In conversation Santayana is reported to have said that Oliver is "the dialectically ultimate Puritan, because he's a man who very conscientiously believes he shouldn't have a conscience."[11] But in the prologue, Santayana also tells us that Oliver had no "timidity or fanaticism or calculated hardness." He felt "hatred of all shams, scorn of all mummeries, a bitter merciless pleasure in the hard facts.

And that passion for reality was beautiful in him. . . . He was a millionaire, and yet scrupulously simple and silently heroic" (14).

This being Santayana's conception of Oliver's character, one might conclude that the novel is basically an attack on puritanism itself. For even its flowering in the fine and exemplary protagonist whom Santayana says he loves, and who represents the young poets whose destruction he grieves, results in tragedy and self-contradiction. The better Oliver is as a human being, in contrast to monstrosities like Uncle Nathaniel, the more his failure to solve the problems of life would reveal the underlying flaw in puritanism as a whole.

But though Santayana's motive may have been partly tendentious in this manner, his admiration for Oliver's purity of soul outweighs any desire to demonstrate the futility of Protestant ideology. Oliver is a tragic hero not only because he cannot escape the contradiction of rejecting puritanism on puritan grounds, but also because he is a spiritual man who cannot reconcile himself to the realm of matter without which he could not exist as a spiritual being, or even as a human being.

This kind of contradiction does not pertain exclusively to any single religious doctrine. It is not peculiar to Protestantism or to puritanism. It is a paradox experienced by everyone who wishes to rise above his or her material nature while being constrained, by the realities of life, to make the attempt only as a product of that nature. In the prologue Santayana compounds the paradox when he remarks that "puritanism is a natural reaction against nature" (14).

Some of the reverberations in this moral dilemma had already been adumbrated in an essay by William James that Santayana must have read. It is called "The Gospel of Relaxation." Addressing himself directly to the young women in his audience, James encourages them to relax their high-minded intensity and to give their personalities greater access to the benefits of freedom and repose. But then James ends his sermon with the following words: "Even now I fear that some of my fair hearers may be making an undying resolve to become strenuously relaxed, cost what it will, for the remainder of her life. It is needless to say that that is not the way to do it. The way to do it, paradoxical as it may seem, is genuinely not to care whether you are doing it or not. Then, possibly, by the grace of God, you may all at once find that you are doing it, and, having learned what the trick feels like, you may (again by the grace of God) be enabled to go on."[12]

The tragedy of Oliver Alden consists in the fact that he was *not* able to do it. Having established this, however, Santayana delves into the psychodynamics—or what might be called the ontodynamics—of his failure. Believing that the being of man is divided into elements of spirit and matter, Santayana observes that these can sometimes be harmonized. In that case, as he says in one of his letters, "*tutti contenti*" (all's well).[13] But when the two orders of being remain in opposition to each other, the tensions between them create a conflict that is inherently tragic. We would trivialize Santayana's thought if we said that Oliver is a moral but largely repressed— above all, sexually repressed—scion of an overly civilized strand of humanity. More important in his tragedy, as Santayana portrays it, is the fact that Oliver wants to live in accordance with natural impulses while also seeking a spiritual vocation that would detach him from the vicissitudes of mere existence. He cannot secure the best of both worlds, and he ends up living in neither.

In the preface Santayana says that Oliver was a spiritual man whose tragedy resulted from his inability to renounce everyday life, as Christ had done, in order to heed his own calling. When Santayana says that Oliver, like the rich young man in the Gospels, would have given his wealth to the poor in order to follow Jesus but then found "no way of salvation to preach" (9), he renews his point about the aridity of American culture. His major insight goes beyond that, however, for he recognizes that tragedy arises from any division within a person's being that prevents him from living in accordance with his own vocation.

In the novel the vicar speaks of two kinds of tragedy: one of the spiritual man, the other of the natural man. He says that the spiritual man must live a tragic life because "his flesh and his pride and his hopes" will have withered early (247). The vicar himself is a tragic figure of this sort, and he rightly intuits that Oliver is also one. Other characters perceive Oliver in the same way: Irma has an image of him as Christ on the Cross, and she identifies his monogram as "the Alpha and Omega of our Saviour" (218); preparatory to rejecting his offer of marriage, his cousin Edith sees him as "one of those rare persons called to a solitary life in a special sense" (468); and earlier he had appeared in a phantasmagoric dream sequence of his own as Gilda, the tragic heroine in Verdi's *Rigoletto* who sacrifices herself in an act of love and spiritual renunciation.

❈

What the vicar says about the tragedy of the natural man is also significant. He is talking primarily of his son Jim, whose capacity to enjoy material pleasures had so greatly impressed Oliver. "The perfection of merely bodily life or of worldly arts is somehow tragic," the vicar declares: "The merely natural man ends tragically, because the spirit in him is strangled" (246, 247). As the novel progresses, Oliver comes to realize how sordid and unsatisfying Jim's life really is despite his powers of enjoyment. Though his experience is totally different from Oliver's and the vicar's, Jim also fails to reconcile the demands of matter and spirit. His failure is symbolized by the image of the black swan. When Oliver first meets him, Jim is the virile captain of the yacht *Black Swan*. He then appears to Oliver as "an ideal elder brother, a first and only friend" (205). By the end of the novel, Oliver suffers not only disillusionment about Jim's character but also grief when Jim is lost at sea. On his way to commiserate with the Darnley family, Oliver is surprised to encounter a black swan in a watery field where none had ever been seen before. What was originally a symbol of beauty surmounting death has now become a symbol of death—in the soul as well as the body—that destroys beauty and does so tragically.

In presenting Oliver and Jim as tragic in these different ways, Santayana scrupulously avoids a moralistic choice between the spiritual and the natural man. These are alternate possibilities for human beings, but each person must decide for himself which best expresses his particular nature. As I have suggested, the only foundation for a good life that Santayana recognizes is the ability to act with self-knowledge about one's nature—one's own individual nature and one's being as a manifestation of human nature in general. In the preface Santayana insists that the sadness of Oliver is not that he died young but that "he stopped himself, not trusting his inspiration." In the essay "A Long Way Round to Nirvana," Santayana asserts that death is neither sad nor tragic in itself. What is truly sad, he says, "is to have some impulse frustrated in the midst of its career, and robbed of its chosen object." In the same place, he tells us that the point in life "is to have expressed and discharged all that was latent in us. . . . The task in any case is definite and imposed on us by nature, whether we recognize it or not."[14]

The tragedies of Oliver and Jim thus result from their inability to realize and to fulfill the diverse potentialities within the nature that each of them had. In Oliver's case the failure is more poignant because, almost to the end of his life, he continues to resist his own spirituality. In a letter, Santayana says that Oliver "was a mystic, touched with a divine consecration. . . . He ought to have been a saint."[15] In making this kind of judgment, Santayana seems to believe that people can learn what their true nature is. And indeed, all of *The Last Puritan* can be seen as Oliver's discovery, through agonizing trial and error, of what he was born to be.

In at least one place, Santayana called his novel the account of a "sentimental education." When the book appeared, critics immediately linked it to *The Education of Henry Adams*. Although it is a tragedy, recording the puritanical self-contradiction that prevented Oliver from carrying out his function as a spiritual man, it also depicts Oliver's progression toward the truth about himself. Having been rejected by Rose because she intuits that he was not made to live in the world like other people and could not love her as a woman wants to be loved, he finally feels liberated from the need to be "commonplace."

Attaining this ultimate awareness, Oliver concludes that there is a divine love to which he can now devote his energies. He believes that it is preferable to whatever earthly love he might have experienced. Without having recourse to any orthodox creed, he sees the direction that his innate calling must take: "We will not accept anything cheaper or cruder than our own conscience. We have dedicated ourselves to the truth, to living in the presence of the noblest things we can conceive. If we can't live so, we won't live at all" (553–54).

The "we" here includes his outlandish Uncle Nathaniel, but Oliver speaks as the embodiment of what is deepest and most fully clarified in the puritanism that they jointly represent. To this extent, Oliver's career is not at all tragic. His subsequent death is wholly irrelevant. In having reached a stage at which he can understand the kind of person he is and has become, he achieves the self-knowledge that Santayana recommends throughout his moral philosophy. Though Oliver fails in life, he has also succeeded: for in knowing himself, he faces up to reality and transcends his own tragedy.

Oliver is not the only character who achieves self-knowledge. Mario also does. Unlike either Oliver or Jim, Mario has nothing in him that could be deemed tragic. Mario is a healthy-minded man, capable of enjoying the usual animal instincts. He is rational and sensible while also being uninhibited and unrepressed. He is a Cherubino as an adolescent, a Don Juan as a young man, and in maturity a functioning husband, father, and pillar of respectability. Without paying much attention to theological matters, he remains an avowed Catholic and even becomes an official at the Vatican. He has an existence that Santayana considers "natural," and we may take Mario's development as indicative of how a well-attuned Latin can cope with American and European life in the twentieth century. At the same time, he cannot be expected to comprehend the nature of someone like Oliver. Whatever Mario may feel for Oliver as a friend, the limitations in his own nature prevent him from understanding the range of potentialities in Oliver's. To have that kind of awareness Mario would need to be a philosopher, and in this novel the only true philosopher is Santayana himself.

In one of his letters Santayana says that Oliver was meant to be unlike him in physical and moral character, but "in the quality of his *mind,* he is what I am or should have been in his place."[16] In his book about Santayana, Cory—who speaks of himself as one of the prototypes of Mario—also identifies Oliver with Santayana. Certainly they are alike in being scholarly types who pursue the truth and eventually withdraw from routine society.

Nevertheless, the differences between Santayana and Oliver are quite pronounced. Santayana regularly enjoyed the good things of this world, and he never claimed to be a spiritual man. In one place he notes that he has "the Epicurean contentment . . . a humourous animal faith in nature and history, and no religious faith. . . . Oliver hadn't this intellectual satisfaction, and he hadn't that Epicurean contentment."[17] From this point of view, Santayana would seem to be closer to Mario than to any of the other characters. Being the older man salvaging his past, Santayana the novelist (like Stendhal before him) appears as the bemused commentator who laughs at his own youthful vitality while also relishing the lovely moments it once afforded. Like Mario, he savored all that European culture had to offer, and he did so by treating his Catholic origins as a resource rather than a burden.

There is one respect, however, in which Mario is not Santayana, except perhaps as a wish fulfillment. Mario's sexual orientation is of a sort that Santayana did not have, though he obviously thought it entirely normal. Hardly anything is known about Santayana's sexuality, but the little that he and others said about it would lead one to believe that his erotic life was different from Mario's. One of the rare bits of evidence occurs in a conversation between Santayana and Cory that is often misquoted. They have been reading the poetry of A. E. Housman, and Santayana remarks:

"I suppose Housman was really what people nowadays call 'homosexual.'"

"Why do you say that?" I protested at once.

"Oh, the sentiment of his poems is unmistakable," Santayana replied.

There was a pause, and then he added, as if he were primarily speaking to himself:

"I think I must have been that way in my Harvard days—although I was unconscious of it at the time."

He said this so naturally that I was not at all startled.

He seemed a little ashamed to confess to having been so innocent. . . .

Santayana then told me that various people at Harvard . . . must have suspected something unusual in his make-up: he felt acutely at times their silent disapproval, and it was one of the things that made him determined to retire from teaching there as soon as he could afford to do so.

"I couldn't stick it any longer than I did. . . . I had even made up my mind that if things got any worse, I would go straight to William James and ask him frankly what it was all about."[18]

In a subsequent footnote, Cory says of Santayana: "If he was a man with the feelings of a woman, he was not aware (until well into middle life) what this might indicate to a Freudian expert. When he did finally suspect something 'unconventional' in his psyche, I am certain it only hardened a predilection to renounce the world as much as was compatible with living a rational life devoted to his labors. . . . He simply considered sex a nuisance; he would never have dreamed of bragging—like André Gide—about an idiosyncrasy in development."[19]

In his biography of Santayana, John McCormick makes a concerted effort to show that Santayana was indeed a homosexual. But the information he adduces would seem to prove little more than the possibility that Santayana occasionally had "erotic friendships." Santayana applies that phrase not to any experience of his own, but to relationships within *The Last Puritan*. The word *love* is often used in the novel to describe what Mario and Oliver feel for each other, and also the strong affective bond that ties Oliver to Jim Darnley. There is no suggestion of a sexual attraction between Mario and Oliver. But Oliver's feelings about Jim are presented as an adolescent crush that could well have had physical overtones. In earlier life Jim was expelled from the Royal Navy because of some name-less sexual "immorality" between himself and other sailors. After his death, Jim's father the vicar says to Oliver: "Jim has made you suffer a great deal for years. . . . You were more deeply attached to Jim than you have ever suspected." To this, Oliver replies: "Yes. That is the truth. I loved him from the beginning" (507, 508).

When the novel first appeared, Santayana expressed surprise to Cory that in the reviews "there are objections repeatedly made to Mario, but not a breath against the ambiguities of Jim. Don't people catch on, or are they shy?"[20] Santayana states in various letters that Jim is modeled on his friend Frank Russell (John Francis Stanley, Second Earl Russell). In *Persons and Places* many pages are devoted to their uneven relationship, revealing Russell's emotional difficul-ties throughout his marriages and love affairs, but also portraying him as an aristocratic and forceful man whose erotic appeal en-tranced Santayana when they initially became friends.[21]

These personal details are worth mentioning because *The Last Puritan* has sometimes been called a "homosexual novel," with the intimation that this defines a limiting perspective from which it is written. But that invokes a mode of classification that is too crude, and too imprecise, for this particular novel. In the preface, as in some of his letters, Santayana admits that he is ill-equipped to write about (heterosexual) romantic love; and in fact, his book includes no examples of it, although Oliver woos first Edith and then Rose in his puritanical manner and certainly hopes that sexual oneness will someday develop. It never does in his case, and the heterosexual experiences of Mario and Jim are problematic in ways that I shall consider later. What remains at the core of the novel is not homo-sexuality but rather friendship as an ideal intimacy. In view of the love that it generally incorporates, it may be called erotic; but noth-ing is gained by reducing it to one or another type of libidinal sex-uality—whether overt or merely "latent," as Freud would say.

It is evident from *Persons and Places* how much friendship meant to Santayana throughout his life: friendship with women as well as men, friendship with schoolmates or others who visited him in later life as well as friendship at a distance and mediated through letter writing. Having no family of his own and very little communal involvement, Santayana found in friendship an essential supplement to the solitude he cultivated and needed for his work. Santayana's philosophy of love is at its strongest when he describes the type of bonding that is not marital or sexual or romantic but rather a life-enhancing affection between friends.

Of the many places in which Santayana discusses the nature of friendship, the account in *Reason in Society* is especially useful for understanding *The Last Puritan*. In a chapter entitled "Free Society" some of his comments about ideal friendship resemble what Aristotle says in the *Nicomachean Ethics*. Emphasizing the importance of similarity with respect to social status and moral aspiration, Santayana claims that friendship involves not only personal liking, or even "animal warmth," but also the pursuit of shared ideals. "The necessity of backing personal attachment with ideal interests is what makes true friendship so rare. It is found chiefly in youth, for youth best unites the two requisite conditions—affectionate comradeship and ardour in pursuing such liberal aims as may be pursued in common."[22]

In the novel, the moments of greatest vibrancy and vividness occur in the scenes that portray Oliver's growing capacity for friendship: on the yacht or watching a football game with Jim, at Eton and later at Harvard with Mario. Oliver's initial hopefulness with respect to Jim dissipates when he comes to realize how greatly their ideals diverge. For all its initial excitement, their affiliation is presented as an incomplete friendship. In contrast, the intimacy and kinship between Oliver and Mario deepen throughout the novel. Though they are temperamentally not the same, their friendship endures and overcomes all obstacles, including the fact that the two young women to whom Oliver proposes marriage reject him partly because they see how inferior he is as a potential lover compared to Mario.

This theme of friendship surmounting the hazards of sexual competition, a theme that Shakespeare exploits in *The Two Gentlemen of Verona,* reaches its climax in the final pages of the novel. Mario visits Rose and her mother in order to communicate the terms of Oliver's will. At one point Rose says that Oliver used to speak of Mario as a lady-killer, but that she can perceive from his grief at Oliver's death that "like almost all other men, you really care for your friends more than for your victims" (563). Mario restrains himself from replying that "there is a love that passeth the love of women," and he fails to see that Rose is implicitly offering herself as a willing victim. But after he leaves the house, the meaning of her remark suddenly strikes him and he toys with the possibility of adding her to his list of conquests. He finally rejects the idea, and Santayana tells us that "the tag of an old French comedy kept running in his head: *Je ne vous aime pas, Marianne; c'était Célio qui vous aimait"* (566).

The play to which Mario alludes is *Les Caprices de Marianne* by Alfred de Musset. It was later to be one of the sources of Renoir's film *La Règle du jeu (The Rules of the Game),* in which Célio—that is, the man of the skies—becomes a transatlantic aviator who is more at home in the clouds than on the ground.[23] Musset's tragicomedy has a structure similar to that of *The Last Puritan:* both are based on the contrasting personalities of two friends, one of whom is pureminded and sky-blue, while the other is a natural man given to the pleasures of lovemaking. The spiritual man having been killed in Musset's play (by henchmen of Marianne's jealous husband), she tells his friend that he is really the one she has loved all along. He spurns her, however, with the words that Santayana incorporates in his novel. In both works male friendship, the authentic bonding between men, prevails over sexual love for women.

Much earlier in the novel, Oliver gives his own ideas about friendship in a brief essay on Plato's *Phaedrus* and *Symposium* that he writes for Santayana's course. He insists that in friendship "there may be love, perhaps the highest and most intense love, but there is not a bit of desire." Oliver does admit that desire may intrude upon friendship, but he insists that this is "mere sensuality" which is driven out "when friendship becomes clear and strong" (420).

Of course, this need not be taken as a definitive statement of Santayana's philosophy. He was a materialist who found in Freud's theories about sex a great deal that seemed quite plausible. He never suggests that friendship can exist without *some* desire. All the same, he generally places friendship and sexual love in very different categories, just as Oliver does. And though some of his own friendships may have been emotionally gratifying, he freely confessed that even his love poetry was based on speculative enthusiasm rather than actual passions. In a letter to an old friend, he says: "Love has never made me long unhappy, nor sexual impulse uncomfortable: on the contrary in the comparatively manageable form in which they have visited me, they have been *great fun*."[24] He then explains that for him love has mainly been "the golden light of diffused erotic feeling" falling upon the otherwise "deadly" world in which he lived.

This attitude toward sexual love is coherent with the thinking of Mario in the novel. Although Mario—unlike Santayana—has enjoyed sexual love on many occasions, he never describes it as romantic ecstasy. For him, as for Jim, lovemaking is a sport that satisfies material appetites. Mario asserts that Oliver's great mistake consisted in regarding all women as ladies without realizing that all ladies are women. He ascribes Oliver's erotic failures to his having had a mother who never loved him and whom he never loved. Mario traces his own success to the fact that his mother has always been the principal object of his affections. He considers this natural because she suckled him and never stopped treating him as her special darling.

That Mario's experience is not the same as Santayana's is clear from those pointed statements in the autobiography about the coldness of his mother and her inability to love her children. Mario's mother is an opera singer who gave up her career in order to devote her artistic talents to the optimal upbringing of the child she loved so much. Generalizing from her example, Mario enunciates the idea that singing, and art in general, resembles and recapitulates the instinct of love in taking us beyond conventional daily life and enabling us to feel what is deepest in our nature. Santayana had said the same in other books. To that extent, Mario is his spokesman. But like Oliver, Santayana also suspected that—despite its imaginative power—sexual love might really be "a mere escape and delusion" (396). This ambivalence recurs in all his philosophy.

In the chapter on love in *Reason in Society*, Santayana presented his views dialectically. He began with the Schopenhauerian reductivism that treats sexual love as an illusory outgrowth of biological imperatives, which determine what is really happening in the human organism. He then combined this materialist approach with the more Platonistic one represented by his concept of idealization: the beloved serves as an image, and possibly a symbol, of some ideal of goodness or beauty that captivates the lover.

By the time he finished *The Last Puritan*, Santayana had already modified this analysis considerably. Mario the natural man sees love as "great fun" and relishes the play of imagination that it involves, but he does not allow his amatory feeling to become a Platonic longing. He seeks for beauty through civilized dalliance and is adept at finding it, without having much interest in idealization as

Santayana used that term. Mario is quite different from the courtly lovers whom Santayana discussed in his early essay "Platonic Love in Some Italian Poets." As for Oliver, he never achieves sexual love for anyone. Though he finally understands the importance of idealization, he assigns it to a divine love that exceeds and defeats whatever hopes he might still have for loving another person sexually.

Oliver's development in this respect is instructive. It parallels the progression in Santayana's philosophy of love. Throughout the novel, Oliver is depicted as disqualified or prevented from experiencing what Rose calls "happy love, natural, irresistible, unreasoning love" (548). But at the end he perceives the meaning of another kind of love that takes on greater importance. Having been freed by Rose's refusal to marry him, he concludes that beyond the kindliness he may have felt for the real Rose, or Edith, or even Jim and Mario, his love for these persons was "only an image, only a mirage, of my own aspiration." Though this mirage may have obscured the reality of the individuals he has loved, "my image of them in being detached from their accidental persons, will be clarified in itself, will become truer to my profound desire; and the inspiration of a profound desire, fixed upon some lovely image, is what is called love" (552).

If we think of the image of one's own aspiration as the instantiation of an ideal beauty that one admires, Oliver's statement resembles what Santayana had been saying about love as early as *Interpretations of Poetry and Religion*. But actually the conception belongs to the thinking about "charity" that Santayana began to develop twenty-five years later in *Dialogues in Limbo* and subsequently completed in *The Realm of Spirit* and *The Idea of Christ in the Gospels*.

In turning away from sexual love, in concluding that only divine love can satisfy him entirely, Oliver continues to reject traditional religious ideas about a divinity toward whom that love must be directed. He still believes that the idea of a supernatural being is just another mirage, "'an impossible object.'" But his culminating insight occurs when he concludes that "the falser that object is, the stronger and clearer must have been the force in me that called it forth and compelled me to worship it. It is this force in myself that matters: to this I must be true" (553).

Many years before, Oliver's father had told him that friendship is a sentiment that belongs to the boyishness of young comrades discovering what the world is like and that eventual disillusionment would transmute the tenderness of friendship into charity. In his ultimate appreciation of the supervening goodness in what he calls divine love, Oliver finds in himself a capacity for charity that reveals the purity of his own spirit. This is the force that matters. Oliver cannot live in accordance with his true nature, and we are expected to believe that even if he had not died young he would have discovered no way to overcome the crippling effects of his puritan heritage. But he is a hero because he does attain this greater clarification about the nature of spirit and the possibility of spiritual love.

How then is spirit elucidated by Santayana's novel? And what can we learn from Oliver's tragedy? Two statements in the novel provide some leverage upon these questions. The first occurs when Oliver recognizes that his aborted love for Rose was a fixation upon an image or mirage within himself. Speaking of all love between human beings, he says: "And the true lover's tragedy is not being jilted; it is being accepted" (552). The other comment is given by Santayana himself in the prologue. He there describes Oliver's secret problem as the tragedy of spirit when it exceeds its need to understand and "wishes to govern" (17).

If we juxtapose these statements and read them both as reflections of Santayana's own philosophy, we could possibly interpret him as meaning that man's existence in the world is not compatible with the ends of spirit, and that spirit is forever doomed to submission and despair. This mode of interpretation distorts the general intentions of Santayana's thought. When he says that Oliver's tragedy resulted from spirit wanting to govern rather than to understand, he refers to the fact—asserted in all his writings—that spirit has no substance of its own. It must always depend on the prior being of matter: it can arise only from material causes that happen to produce it in some animate creature. Spirit is lodged within the organic and vegetative structure that Santayana, following Aristotle in the *De Anima,* calls psyche.

On Santayana's view, only psyche can effect changes in the actual world. Psyche is a part of matter, a bit of living substance within the fields of force that cause all things to exist or not exist. As the exotic by-product of psyche, spirit is the light of consciousness or awareness that can reflect about its surroundings, that can attend to qualities or essences presented to it, that can contemplate beauty in all its aspects, that can condemn what it sees and hope for something better, and that can even aspire toward ideal accomplishments. But Santayana maintains that spirit has no power and must be distinct from the sources of power, since they belong to matter as the sole reality that determines the nature of everything existent. Oliver has a tragic life because he cannot accept this dependency of spirit. Had he done so, he would have recognized the authority of matter—as Mario does—and felt no need to constrain his instinctual drives or desires.

When Oliver says that the true lover's tragedy is in being accepted rather than rejected, he expresses a despairing sentiment that one finds in other books of Santayana. But his negativistic remarks should not be taken out of context. There is a dynamic within Santayana's dialectic. Far from precluding the human possibility of reconciliation between matter and spirit, he merely portrays the great difficulty in attaining it. This then serves as a preliminary to understanding the true dimensions of that grand achievement. In Mario's ability to sample the varied consummations that nature affords, spirit is also present. It occurs in his playfulness, his imaginative wit, his sensitivity to beauty, and in general his capacity to enjoy the spectacle of pervasive materiality to which he is permanently faithful without wholly identifying himself with it. Detachment of this sort, which is essential if spirit is to be free, does not prevent Mario from living in the world and taking action for the sake of what he loves.

I am not saying that Mario is Santayana's ideal. He contributes to it in a way that the other characters cannot, but there are heights of spirituality that Mario will never approximate. As a man who has learned to accept his material being within the confines of civilization, Mario has little yearning for purity. Yet spirit, as Santayana interprets it, longs for self-purification. It feels a need to renounce the world once it learns that it cannot govern it. What Santayana calls "the spiritual life" is spirit seeking to disintoxicate itself from everything that is imperfect in our existence. Santayana is certain that the effort cannot succeed, and he uses the example of Caleb Wetherbee, as well as Uncle Nathaniel and the vicar, to illustrate the aberrations to which it can lead. At the same time, Santayana also admires the fearless integrity with which these twisted persons crave their own austere purgation. Suffering in a world that spirit never made, the spiritual man responds to the tragedy of human factuality by proudly and defiantly rejecting all compromising imperfections.

The ideal for Santayana would be a composite of Mario and Oliver. For then the two forms of spirit could be united in perfect harmony: spirit as an exuberant light that plays upon the waters of natural possibilities, and spirit as the spirituality that seeks purification while beweeping its outcast state within a universe that is ultimately meaningless. Neither is sufficient by itself.

❊

Santayana devotes 40 percent of his novel to the ancestry and boyhood of Oliver Alden. The influence of puritanism is obvious throughout his early education, but the effect of Romantic paganism must not be ignored. It is transmitted through Irma the governess, who admires—as Santayana also did—the writings of Goethe and Schopenhauer. Though Caleb Wetherbee calls Goethe a "diabolical guide for the soul," Oliver has already been convinced by Irma that Goethe understood the beauty of living in accordance with nature. But Irma also communicates Goethe's insistence upon renunciation: "*Entbehren sollst Du, sollst entbehren!*" She is thus both a servant and subverter of the puritan creed. The division in Oliver's soul is already present in her formation of him.

Something similar applies to the Schopenhauerian influence. Irma teaches her pupil that Schopenhauer is "a most wonderful idealist" who believes that everything becomes enchanted once we "suspend our Will." She neglects to point out that Schopenhauer also thinks the will in us is a manifestation of a cosmic will that is purely material, deterministic, and omnipotent despite our desire to suspend it. In willing not to will, we undertake a paradoxical effort that Schopenhauer depicts as ultimately unavailing, even though he recommends it.

Oliver's puritan struggle renews this metaphysical paradox. In one of her letters Irma laments, inconsistently, that Peter Alden makes "*il gran rifiuto*" (the great refusal), which she calls "treason to life." In Oliver's father the energy of life has diminished to a point where the rejecting of it seems relatively trivial. In Oliver, however, the contrasting forces in the paradox remain sufficiently powerful to make their mutual opposition symbolic of the human tragedy. Oliver is heroic in refusing to deny or to falsify the fundamental conflict he feels within himself. He grapples with it persistently, but he knows there is no solution.

The dualism that Santayana establishes between the spiritual and the natural may also be approached through his ideas about agapē and eros. In *The Realm of Spirit* he briefly discusses these concepts without having any hope that theology can eliminate the philosophical problems to which they lead.[25] Thirty-five years earlier, in *Reason in Religion,* he had recounted Augustinian notions about the two cities of God. In that book he presented the separation between nature and spirituality as a poetic fable that was more persuasive as myth or moral insight than as literal doctrine.

The Last Puritan uses explicit fiction as a further device for exploring traditional ideas about eros and agapē. Through eros men and women seek what is good for them as individuals and generically as a member of the human race. This good they find in empirical nature but also in that which creates and continually sustains empirical nature. Eros defines that much of love which is appraisive, acquisitive, and self-oriented, though not necessarily selfish since the enlightened soul realizes that it can perfect itself through acts that benefit others. Agapē pertains to human spirit in a way that eros does not, insofar as agapē is creative bestowal that originates with a wholly spiritual deity who is already perfect and has no need to acquire goodness.

As young men who belong to a particular moment in time, Oliver and Mario are more than just personifications of the attempt to harmonize agapē and eros. They are not allegorical figures. The concepts are nevertheless in them, much as determinism or evolution or instinct are also in them. We understand them better as representations of human beings because of the relevant concepts, and through their fictional behavior they show how abstract ideas can elucidate potentialities common to us all.

Henry James had also used concepts such as these to dramatize the differences between his characters. Milly Theale is a spiritual person of the sort that Oliver Alden tries to be: she descends with the wings of a dove in acts of self-sacrifice that show forth the nature of divine agapē. The recipients of her love, Merton Densher and Kate Croy, are not as carefree in their search for appetitive goods as Mario, but they are like him in revealing the workings of eros in the natural world.

If we were to compare the aesthetic excellence of these two novels, we might have difficulty deciding which is greater. Received opinion nowadays would certainly place *The Wings of the Dove* on a higher plane than *The Last Puritan*. But the literary style of James's novel, above all in the crucial pages at the end, is often clumsy and inferior. Like much of James's writing in his final period, whole paragraphs are overwritten and poorly phrased. The book has little of the luminosity or clarity of thought that appears in every line of Santayana's novel. Oscar Wilde complained that James wrote fiction as if it were a painful duty. One could not say that about *The Last Puritan*. If *The Wings of the Dove* is nevertheless a better novel, this results from its heightened dramatic structure. When Milly not only forgives but also shelters the friends who have betrayed her, we feel the purity and intensity of her love to a degree that cannot be matched by anything in Santayana's book. Oliver eventually understands that he has a spiritual calling, but he never fulfills it in an adequate or conclusive act. Almost perversely, Santayana seems to thwart the possibility of empathy or catharsis on the part of the reader.

This avoidance of moralistic melodrama is central to Santayana's intention. Although Oliver's life manifests a tragic failing in himself, in puritanism, and in American culture, his death is insignificant. Milly's dying gesture is fully dramatic, and her pitiable condition moves us far more than Oliver's. But his story is a tragedy, and hers is not. If we consider James's novel greater than Santayana's, perhaps it is because we prefer being stirred emotionally by a work of fiction that shows how death can provide a moral and even saintly triumph rather than being a natural termination that has little impact in the universe. Santayana forces us to take that as fundamental.

In the prologue and the epilogue, which are parts of the fiction as much as the story itself, Santayana appears in a cameo role discussing with Mario first the memoir they agree that he should write and then the sense and value of what he has actually written. The preface, which Santayana added for the Triton edition of his works two years after the novel was published, is a piece of literary criticism that he might have written about someone else's novel.

Much earlier he had done something comparable in relation to his philosophical tragedy *Lucifer*, a work that addresses many of the same themes as *The Last Puritan*. When the editors of the *Harvard Monthly* told him they could not find anyone to review *Lucifer*, Santayana offered to contribute a notice himself. It appeared, signed H.M., as a sympathetic analysis of his play that nevertheless included harsh criticism. Throughout the novel, Santayana employs literary criticism as a part of his narrative technique. Since the characters ordinarily reenact aspects of himself, they are embodiments of his own dialectically disparate ideas about the verbal arts he knew and practiced. While speaking in the literate manner which is Santayana's authorial voice, they use his varied responses to works of literature as a means of defining their personal individuality.

Like many other novelists, James avoided this device because he feared that the talkiness in such discursive prose would slacken the momentum of his dramatic fables and prevent them from reaching the focus or sharpened resolution in which they usually culminate. But Santayana was experimenting with a different kind of novel, one that portrays a spiritual education that unfolds progressively without depending upon a succession of ethical choices or decisions like the ones in the typical Jamesian plot. To demonstrate the division in Oliver's soul, Santayana did not need to have the opposing forces confront each other through momentous scenes or situations. He was more interested in analyzing the forces themselves and showing whence they had arisen. The discursiveness that would have been ruinous for James is therefore no deterrent in Santayana's novel, any more than it is in Proust's.

In James the characters often finish each other's sentences and seem to read one another's mind with great facility. This provides a unity of communication that typifies the small and highly integrated society in which they all live. With that as a premise, James can then construct the moral and emotional dilemmas that become the contrapuntal foreground in his novels. In Santayana the unitary setting for everything that happens to and in the characters is the world as a place where man must find his salvation as a partly material, partly spiritual being. James never undertook an overall theme of this magnitude. In doing so, Santayana remains faithful to his own vision while also recognizing the demands of creative fiction. If the characters all belong to his thinking about reality, it is by analogy to the way in which, as Spinoza would say, everything that exists reflects and participates in the totality which is God the Creator.

Santayana's identification with Oliver and with Mario requires no further demonstration. Nor is it necessary to show how much the vicar or Irma or even Jim repeats ideas that Santayana develops in other books. The degree to which Oliver's father articulates problems that are indigenous to Santayana is more likely to be overlooked. In most of the novel, Peter Alden serves as a parody of the rich American wastrel wandering aimlessly around the globe. He may also be seen as an ostracized sinner like the Wandering Jew or the Flying Dutchman, since he has killed a man in Boston. But even that is presented as the accidental consequence of a college lark. Shortly before his death, however, Peter has conversations with Oliver that penetrate to the heart of Santayana's philosophy.

At the time, father and son are living in England and visiting Eton, where Peter has had a physical breakdown. Oliver is eighteen years old; he is due to return to America and enter the freshman class at college. As a man of spirit in process of development, he has already withdrawn from arbitrary allegiance to conventional beliefs and "home prejudices": "He had vowed himself to universal sympathy, understanding, and justice" (306). Like his father, though independently, Oliver has concluded that one does best to fulfill one's own nature while letting others live as they wish. Despite their Calvinist origins, both father and son profess an underlying sympathy with all of nature, and they repudiate traditional dogmas about an objective order that could indicate how anyone else should live. Yet here in Eton, Peter instructs his son about Jacob's ladder as the biblical image that sustains English aristocracy.

Peter recognizes that Jacob's ladder is only a manufactured ideal of hierarchical approaches to perfection. He calls it "the fabulous moral order imposed on the universe by the imagination of Cousin Caleb and Plato and conservative Anglican gentlemen"; and he states that the "heathen imagination in Goethe and Emerson and you and me, and in your liberal British intellectuals and philosophers, has outgrown that image" (302). But still he greatly respects Eton's snobbish and repressive adherence to moral rigidities symbolized by Jacob's ladder. He approves of this as an orientation based on a myth that is true to human nature even if the universe itself affords no objective authority for anything of the sort.

Oliver is unconvinced by his father's exposition. He wants to know how one can justify a preference among different possibilities if one has sympathy toward all of them and none can claim any prior validity. At this point his father drifts off into a digression, and neither he nor Oliver can do much with the issues posed by ethical relativism. Nor does Santayana himself. Like the vicar, he merely tells us to "choose with true self-knowledge," and in his other writings he makes only scattered attempts to solve this kind of problem. In the novel he leaves the matter wholly unresolved. It nevertheless precipitates the deliberation that leads to Peter's decision to commit suicide.

In killing himself, Oliver's father takes action that approximates the dovelike gesture of Milly Theale. To some extent he plays the coward, as he has throughout his life, but also he is motivated by a love of others: "My disappearance now will liberate everybody: Jim can have his money, Oliver can salve his conscience, Harriet [his wife] can have her way. The last action of my life will be the kindest—kindest to others and kindest to myself" (318–19).

The death of Peter Alden occurs close to the midpoint of the novel. It marks an ending to the boyhood of Oliver and the beginning of his manhood. It is an event that Oliver later duplicates when he stops himself emotionally, though not literally through suicide, having found no viable exit from his self-division. He too acts with kindness in arranging for the financial well-being of everyone he has touched who needs money—Mario, Rose, Jim's illegitimate son, Mrs. Darnley. In his case, however, death completes a tragedy, whereas his father merely finishes a life that was partly farcical and partly a prolonged search for blissful nothingness. One might say that this too is a tragedy. But we do not experience it as such because we never see Peter struggling or seeking to master his destiny.

That is what Oliver does from beginning to end. It is what makes him a tragic hero and raises him above his father, or the vicar, or Jim, or all the other failures in the novel.

The meditation that eventuates in Peter's suicide centers about the character of his son. In his craving for universal sympathy, Oliver understands that this involves freedom from conventional restraints. If he is true to his own nature, he will not conform to the merely routine expectation that he must return home and enter college. He can choose instead to stay in Europe and take care of his ailing father. Peter considers this the bold and independent action that would liberate his son from self-destructive conformity. But Peter senses that Oliver's "petrified conscience" prevents him from acting freely or "reshaping his duty in a truer harmony with his moral nature" (317). Without the support that Oliver might have provided, Peter discovers in himself nothing that would enable him to go on living.

Throughout the novel we see Oliver striving not only for ideal rectitude in accordance with the truth but also for the highest love that human beings are capable of attaining in their natural state. At the end he clarifies his thinking about this kind of love, and at earlier stages we see him groping toward such clarification. When he visits the Darnley family in Oxford for the first time, he wonders whether people would love one another more or less if they knew absolutely everything about each other. St. Augustine, whom Santayana does not mention, had in fact argued that the greatest love requires total knowledge. Oliver concludes that such knowledge might be saddening and even terrifying but that it would enable us to "understand the irresistible bent of all sorts of creatures even when this bent was fatal to them or to ourselves" (277). Oliver progresses toward this superior love, but we never see him reaching it. Except in his friendship with Mario, the love he does experience is neither happy nor fulfilling.

In his parting poem to Rose, Oliver says that their relationship illustrates "the pity, not the joy, of love" (562). Santayana repeats these words in the preface, using them to describe Oliver's career in its entirety. Though he never portrays adequate or truly satisfying love, Santayana recognizes what prevents it from occurring. In the prologue he says that the erotic "impediment" in Oliver and in the ladies Oliver knew resulted from their failure to harmonize sex and love: "Sex for them becomes simply a nuisance, and they can't connect it pleasantly with their feeling for the people they love. Therefore sensuality for them remains disgusting, and tenderness incomplete" (16).

Oliver cannot eradicate that disability. In effect, it reduces to the split between lust and love that Freud discusses in "The Most Prevalent Form of Degradation in Erotic Life" (also known as "On the Universal Tendency to Debasement in the Sphere of Love").[26] It is related to a split that Santayana himself perpetuates in his ambivalence between materialism and Platonism. He does not overcome this intellectual impediment any more than Oliver can. If any of his characters could do so, it would be Mario; but he lacks the intellectual acumen needed for that achievement.

The concept of love that Oliver finally intuits, and that Santayana examines throughout his last books, is not sexual love. It is only a love that reveals what the human spirit is capable of attaining in its most elevated moments. It is, moreover, a love that Santayana normally depicts in its pitiful rather than its joyful aspects. This is understandable in view of his belief that all existence must be ephemeral and ultimately meaningless. In one of his letters he says that "the world is not a tragedy or a comedy: it is a flux."[27] If that is true, nothing can amount to very much.

At the same time, Santayana's writings teach us how we can turn our ontological misfortune into self-awareness, free entertainment, and comic relief. What he does not show, or fully comprehend, is the possibility that men and women can sometimes achieve a gratifying love for one another that combines spiritual aspiration with a quest for sexual harmony. This kind of love, when it succeeds, is neither pitiful nor tragic but rather a consummatory oneness that is able to provide its own inherent joy. Santayana tells us little about it.

In *The Last Puritan* there is no character who coordinates the different tendencies of our being. There is none who manifests the harmonization between spirit and matter. Though Santayana's critics were mistaken in thinking that he believed the spiritual life superior to the rational one or that he advocated asceticism and quietistic withdrawal from society, they were right in sensing his skepticism about the usual attempts to resolve basic problems of humanity. Some of the characters in the novel are "good people," as he insists in one of his letters, but none of them fulfills the potentialities of his or her goodness, or appears as a complete individual.

Perhaps that is why many readers have felt that Santayana treats his characters like marionettes that merely express his various views about the world. Santayana declares in several places that the characters are real to him and that throughout the years they have spoken within his inner monologue like actual people. This is plausible, and entirely compatible with their being pieces of Santayana's mind. For his mind, as well as his personality, was radically pluralistic within the categories he imposes. He is not only Oliver and Mario, or each as the alter ego of the other, but also Oliver's father. Peter Alden is a homeless and itinerant aesthete much as Santayana was. He is what Santayana could have been if he had had great wealth, a willingness to make a conventional marriage, and no creative talent.

Since these are such vast differences, one might wonder how the two men are alike at all. The point is that, despite his weakness of character and ability, Peter Alden is an enlightened spirit and a naturalist in philosophy who manifests Santayana's pessimism, resignation, and sophisticated detachment. But there is nothing—not even the nothingness of nirvana—in which Alden believes. If Santayana could point to the idealized fusion of Mario and Oliver and say, "That's what I would like to have been in my youth," so too could he say of Peter Alden, "That's what I, in my alienated condition, might have become."

On each occasion on which the characters of *The Last Puritan* discuss famous authors and literary works, their opinions are both their own and also Santayana's. Jim describes *Hamlet* as "a rum old play, full of bombast and absurdities, but with a lot of topping lines in it," while Oliver asserts that Hamlet was "tremendously pure and superior to all cut-and-dried opinions of ordinary people and even of science. This was what rendered him unfit for the everyday world" (229, 230). Santayana had taken both positions himself in earlier essays. The same is true of disputes among the characters about Whitman, Goethe, Homer, and others. In our present age of relativism and deconstruction, this recurrent device will neither baffle nor dismay. But we have to realize that Santayana generally agrees with all of the contrasting opinions. They articulate his own diversified perspective.

Through this systematic ricochet Santayana seeks to overcome the residual alienation that permeates his writing. In *The Last Puritan* the dichotomies appear not only in the contrast between Oliver and Mario—the spiritual and the natural man—but also between Nathaniel and Peter Alden. The brothers embody different inclinations of the Protestant soul in nineteenth-century Boston. Oliver eventually perceives his kinship with Uncle Nathaniel, but he has none of his grotesque fixations; Mario succeeds as a lover of life in ways that Peter would have appreciated but could never emulate. Nathaniel is a freak, and Peter becomes addicted to drugs. The next generation is thus an advance on the previous one. In Oliver's case, however, the burden of the past is a staggering load. It engenders the tragedy.

It also gives rise to the farcical elements in this novel. Except for Aunt Caroline and the boatman Denis Murphy, neither of whom plays a major role, all the older characters are presented as distortions of nature, and therefore more or less ludicrous. Santayana's love for caricature is irresistible to him. He is extreme in the names he gives to minor personages: there is not only Head (lawyer), Hart (minister), and Hand (doctor), but also the Misses Lamb, Doe, Swan, and Bird (friends of Oliver's mother), as well as Mark Lowe (who runs a camp for backward boys and teaches them not to aim too high), Mr. Bowler the pubkeeper, Madame Gorgorini the opera singer, Aïda de Lancey the floozy actress, and so on. From the point of view of spirit, almost any human interest can easily turn into caricature. There is no reality that is better than the one we experience in nature, but spirit realizes that all existence, including the spiritual life, appears ridiculous when it magnifies its own importance.

With this in mind, we should recognize the extent to which *The Last Puritan* is a comedy as well as a tragedy. Though the book is primarily a history of tragic incompleteness, Santayana weaves many satiric and parodistic strands throughout the tapestry of this theme. Among the Greek deities, Hermes—god of wit and comic inventiveness—is the one to whom Santayana pays tribute most of all. Dickens was possibly his favorite novelist. He delighted in the geniality of Dickensian humor mingled, as it is, with ridicule of all pomposity and hypocrisy.

Oliver's mother, his governess, and even his father—to say nothing of the lesser characters—often serve comedic ends. Although as individuals they are sometimes sketched at great length, they provide amusing vistas into the absurdist world through which Oliver must wend his puritan way. The ludicrous, even grotesque traits of these characters intrigue us because we see them from the Olympian vantage of Santayana's cutting insights. His epigrammatic wisdom makes us feel that we too can share his great amusement in observing, at a comfortable distance, the foibles and stupidities of other people.

This display is not always pleasant to watch. In giving us access to it, Santayana may often seem cruel and possibly malicious. More generally, however, tragic and comic elements in his novel spring from a goodwill not totally dissimilar from the one that Santayana admired in Dickens. In his essay about Dickens, Santayana states: "Love of the good of others is something that shines in every page of Dickens with a truly celestial splendour. . . . How generous is this keen, light spirit, how pure this open heart!"[28] If we said the same of Santayana's coruscating thrusts, we would be guilty of gross exaggeration. He is too severe a critic, and too unrelenting in his delineation of human imperfection, to be called an "open heart." Nevertheless, he is far from being heartless or unfeeling. In his sympathetic but unsentimental manner, he reveals an aspect of spirit that may be taken as the final stage in all his thinking.

I am referring to something in Plato's philosophy that Oliver touches on in his college essay. After having first claimed that Plato "knew nothing" about love, Oliver concludes that Plato may have been right after all in identifying love with desire for the Absolute Idea of the Beautiful—"if this means perfection for every creature after its own kind." Oliver then writes, "We can never feel in our own persons the ecstatic bliss of being a perfect porpoise or a perfect eagle. But reason in us may correct our human prejudices and may convince us that other forms of life are as desirable for other creatures as our own form of life is for us" (420).

What Oliver here calls reason Santayana's mature philosophy usually describes as spirit that has reached the ability to love all things as they are in themselves. He does not mean that they are to be loved in their accidental being or for the sake of what they happen to want at any moment. For him, as for Spinoza, they are to be loved as fellow beings—however appalling they may seem—that are straining for some perfection toward which they are separately impelled, each in its own way and all with an equal aspiration to goodness. This is what Santayana identifies as the ability "to love the love in [everything]."[29]

Few people in what we consider the real world attain this kind of love. The characters in The Last Puritan fare no better than the rest of us. Oliver understands the goal but never reaches it. The others ignore it or else delude themselves about its implications. I have no way of knowing whether Santayana thought that he himself approached the ideal he had in mind. But regardless of what his capacities may have been, The Last Puritan is an epiphany of his spirit, and a testament to spirit everywhere. It is a supreme consummation of Santayana's world, as he lived it in youth and as he remembered it in old age. In its plenitude as a work of art, it radiates the poetic and philosophic genius that pervades everything Santayana wrote. It reveals, to paraphrase the last sentence of the epilogue, what the human spirit can "still call its own without illusion."[30]

4 Idealization: Santayana versus Freud

FOR SANTAYANA, as for Plato, all love worthy of the name must have an "ideal object." Lovers seek in each other the embodiment of "an ideal form essentially eternal and capable of endless embodiments."[1] This "form," or "essence" as Santayana later called it, is the abstract possibility of some perfection. If a man falls in love with a fair-haired woman, he does so because his heart has been captured by the ideal of a perfect blonde. It is this ideal object, not the woman "in her unvarnished and accidental person," that the man truly loves. And as the man loves a woman for the sake of an ideal that she suggests, so too does he love ideals for the sake of "the principle of goodness" that gives all goods their ultimate meaning.[2]

Although this much of Santayana's philosophy is Platonistic, it seems closer to Renaissance interpretations of Plato than to Plato himself. In any event, Santayana supplements his Platonism with a naturalistic theory of value. Unlike Plato, he refuses to accord the ideal objects of love an independent status in reality. In being essences, they are all eternal as possibilities, but their ideality consists in the fact that men and women *use* them to guide their conduct. Like other naturalists, Santayana analyzes value in terms of human desire: people want certain things in order to survive or satisfy an interest, and these they call "good." By extrapolating beyond the goods that are actually available in nature, humankind brings ideals into existence as part of its struggle with the environment. By means of imagination, which Santayana emphasizes throughout, we envisage possibilities that would endlessly delight if only they could be had.

According to Santayana, however, these perfections must always remain unattainable. They are merely essences that lead us on; they cannot be realized and would not be perfect if they were. In effect, the ideal objects are but the product of aspiration itself. They issue from the imagination of creatures who live in the realm of matter as well as in the realm of spirit. Expressing a natural impulse but seeking perfections that transcend all existent beings, love is both Platonistic and naturalistic: "There can be no philosophic interest in disguising the animal basis of love, or in denying its spiritual sublimations, since all life is animal in its origin and all spiritual in its possible fruits."[3]

In the past there have been other (and purer) versions of Platonism; but Santayana's is outstanding because of its reliance upon the faculty of imagination. Without imagination, in Santayana though *not* in Plato, there could be no love. Imagination not only fabricates human ideals but also enables one to subsume the beloved under them. This latter function Santayana calls "idealisation." In accordance with its animal base, love originates in instinct. But instinct alone falls short of what Santayana means by love. He says that love always requires the idealizing of what otherwise would be only an object in nature.

Santayana speaks of men and women being propelled toward one another by material forces that control their appetites, their desires, their sexual inclinations. He then goes on to show how different all this is once love intervenes. In an imaginative act the lover experiences the beloved as a reminder of some ideal object that he or she approximates. The lover's love expresses a dual devotion: first to some relevant ideal, itself an effect of human imagination; and second to the beloved, who is valued as the partial embodiment of that beauty or goodness. By treating the beloved as the epiphany of an ideal, the lover dignifies this person beyond the adventitious properties that constitute his or her natural condition. In Santayana's terminology the lover idealizes the beloved, and does so by means of imagination.

For Santayana, then, love is a creative search for unattainable ideal objects. No human being, or even Venus de Milo, can perfectly exhibit the qualities that have evolved as an ideal of female beauty. This ideal object does not exist. It belongs to the realm of essence, where it has been nurtured by a formal genesis that transmutes the natural into an idea of perfection. But when a man loves a woman, Santayana says, his imagination idealizes her in the sense that it allows her to represent the ideal, ignoring her shortcomings for the sake of enjoying whatever perfections he sees in her regardless of how imperfectly she embodies them.

In this fashion love *changes* a sexual object, making it into one that has been idealized. What was formerly a striving for instinctual gratification now becomes an imaginative yearning for perfection, and in further transmutations the instinctual interest may even disappear. After all, it was only an animal prod, though in the order of nature a necessary prelude to love. In the final analysis, Santayana remains a Platonist at heart. As he defines it, love may succeed in idealizing another person, but it is only the ideal itself that anyone *really* loves.

Freud also characterized love as "idealization." But by this he meant something very different from what the Platonists had in mind. Since Santayana mediates between Platonism and naturalism, a discussion of Freud's concept of idealization will help us understand Santayana's. Freud equates idealization with "overestimation" or "overvaluation" of a sexual object. Words like *sex* and *sexual* he uses very broadly. Occasionally they signify instinctual and overt desire for coitus. More often, however, they refer to interests that may conduce to sexuality in the narrow sense but need not be genital in themselves. Through sublimation the erotic instinct may even be directed toward an aim quite remote from sexual intercourse. The motivation will still be sexual in the narrow sense, Freud maintains, but because the instinctual aim has been deflected or inhibited, its true character need never show itself. The objects of a sublimated interest are most easily idealized, and Freud thinks of love as generally aim-inhibited to some extent. Even when the sexual instinct has not been sublimated, the overestimation of the object is "only in the rarest cases" limited to the genitals. Overvaluation applies to every aspect of the body and personality of the beloved, to "all sensations emanating from the sexual object." The phenomenon itself Freud describes as follows, in passages from several works that fit together coherently:

Idealization is a process that concerns the [sexual] *object;* by
it that object, without any alteration in its nature, is aggran-
dized and exalted in the subject's mind.[4] The subject becomes, as it were, intellectually infatuated (that is, his powers
of judgment are weakened) by the mental achievements and
perfections of the sexual object and he submits to the latter's
judgments with credulity.[5] [In] overvaluation . . . the loved
object enjoys a certain amount of freedom from criticism,
and . . . all its characteristics are valued more highly than
those of people who are not loved. . . . If the sensual impul-
sions are somewhat more effectively repressed or set aside,
the illusion is produced that the object has come to be sen-
sually loved on account of its spiritual merits, whereas on
the contrary these merits may really only have been lent to
it by its sensual charm. . . . The tendency which falsifies
judgment in this respect is that of *idealization.*[6]

Freud maintains that idealization, the overvaluation of the beloved,
arises when a child's narcissistic love is first transferred from the self
to another sexual object. Since it is really oneself one wishes to love,
sexual overvaluation of something else appears to Freud as "a state
suggestive of a neurotic compulsion, which is thus traceable to an
impoverishment of the ego as regards libido in favor of the love-
object."[7] The libido Freud describes as a quantity of energy (sexual in the broadest sense) that may be piped to any object. The more
it is channeled away from the self, as in sexual overestimation of another person, the less there remains for the ego of the lover. Normal love, what Freud calls "true object-love," must therefore be an
impoverishment of the self. It is not only an "illusion" and a "logical blinding" about the reality of the beloved, but also a waste of
energy as if it were indeed a neurotic compulsion.

Analyzed in these terms, love would seem to be psychologically hopeless. But Freud also believes that the libido may flow back from other people as well as out to them. This opens new, and more constructive, possibilities. As the self develops, the pressures of external realities force it to give up its primary narcissism. By identifying with these outside demands, a boy or girl constructs what Freud calls an "ego ideal." That is the child's conception of what one should be. Because the ego ideal originates as a yielding to repressive forces in the environment, it drains away libido much as the loved object might; but as the child internalizes the ego ideal, he or she uses it to attain a new kind of narcissistic love. By fulfilling their ideals, men and women restore to themselves the sense of importance, even omnipotence, that the infant had.

This concept of love owes much to Platonistic ideas about harmonious union. But no Platonist or Neoplatonist such as Santayana can accept the Freudian doctrine as it stands. Freud himself merely confused matters when he claimed that what psychoanalysis calls sexuality in the wider sense coincides with "the all-inclusive and all-preserving eros of Plato's *Symposium*."[8] Platonic eros is the desire for that absolute good or beauty which Plato considered objectively real, logically prior to everything that exists, eternal, unchanging, and perfectly unitary. Platonic eros searches for *the* ideal, of which there can be only one, as there is only one universe and one reality. Freudian eros, however, is just libidinal energy programmed by biological necessity, generating whatever ego ideals the environment requires, polymorphously perverse except as repression channels it, similar to instinct in other animals and in no sense transcendental.

In his own fashion Santayana tries to incorporate the outlook of both Freud and Plato. He resembles Freud in owing more to nineteenth-century romanticism than either he or Freud (both reacting against it) realized. Like Freud, Santayana treats values as merely data within the world of nature; and like him too, Santayana derives all ideals from human interest in the sense that nothing could be an ideal except in relation to some need or desire. Santayana's ideal objects are just imagined satisfactions, and authoritative only as human beings choose to make them so.

The Platonistic side of Santayana's philosophy separates it from Freudian analysis. Once they have been chosen, Santayana's ideal objects function as goals that cannot be reduced to any other kind of gratification. They emanate from imagination much as Freud's ego ideals emerge from the libido, but they are not devices for restoring a primal condition of narcissism. Nor are they really dependent upon imagination for their being. As essences, they enjoy the same timeless independence as all logical possibilities. Imagination lights upon them, making them graphic to aspiration and so enabling them to *serve* as ideals; but like the Platonic forms, they are what they are, whether or not a person wishes to follow their guidance. The ideal objects are autonomous perfections, relative to some interest without being reducible to any. They are certainly not reducible to self-love.

According to Santayana, ideal objects are the irreducible ends of spirituality, the perfections to which human beings devote themselves insofar as they belong to the realm of spirit as well as to the realm of matter. Ideals are not objective in the way that Plato thought, for Santayana recognizes that each of us must choose our own in accordance with our personal inclinations. But neither are they substitutes for biological satisfaction. They are not explicable in terms of infant needs, and only in the order of causation do they depend on anything like the libido. The consummations they offer are not instinctual, but are distinctively human nevertheless.

As a result, Santayana's concept of idealization is really quite remote from Freud's, despite their superficial similarity. Freud believes that only persons who fulfill infantile conditions of narcissism, either directly or indirectly, can be idealized. That the beloved should be uniquely irreplaceable he explains by reference to the child's experience with its mother.[9] From this it follows that loving anyone other than the mother can only be idealization in the sense of *over*estimation, *over*valuation, blinded judgment, excessive credulity. We cannot bring back the goddess of our childhood; and since that is how the Freudian lover must perceive the beloved, love can only involve illusion, even delusion—in any event, some fault of reasoning.

For Santayana, however, love need not be irrational. As an act of imagination, it enables us to see the beloved under the aspect of an ideal, to respond to him or her as an image or symbol of possible perfection without necessarily being deceived. As in Plato love is the striving for ultimate goodness, so too does Santayana use it to illustrate how "human reason lives by turning the friction of material forces into the light of ideal goods."[10] Where Freud is a debunker, concerned to show that human values have no significance beyond the libidinal circumstances in which they occur, Santayana accords reason and imagination—in general, the life of spirit—an ambiguous independence. Ideals develop in the course of nature and depend on it for material support; but in revealing what people want, they disclose new possibilities, conceivable goods not deducible from any prior condition. These envisaged goals of aspiration may lead at any time to the future evolution of our species.

What Santayana calls the "pure heart" says: "I love, I do not ask to be loved." On Freud's analysis, such dedication to an ideal can only be a disease of the mind, an intellectual confusion cunning in its ecstasies but obscuring one's real desires. Santayana's Neo-

platonism seeks to exceed any such naturalism, whether or not it is
Freudian.

❈

On one crucial point, Santayana and Freud are very much alike:
they both reduce the love of persons to something else. For Freud,
loving another person comes down to self-love, and every beloved
must be a mere substitute for the mother who loved us when we
were incapable of loving anyone but ourselves. For Santayana, the
beloved is a replica of some chosen perfection to which we dedi-
cate ourselves and for the sake of which we submit to the accidental person through whom it shines. And as Freud wishes to
disintoxicate us from an overvalued object that can only befuddle
the intellect, so too does Santayana recommend an "abstraction
from persons" that is essential for loving the ideal: "Too much sub-
jection to another personality makes the expression of our own
impossible, and the ideal is nothing but a projection of the demands
of our imagination."[11] Both Freud and Santayana address themselves to the same question: "What is it that the lover really desires
in another person?" Freud thinks it is always access to primal narcissism; Santayana thinks it must be an approach to imagined goodness or beauty.

I have no alternative answer to offer. Instead, I suggest there is
something wrong with the question itself. It seems to ask about love
but is really limited to desire. Yet loving is not the same as desiring.
We desire things or persons for what they can give us, for satisfactions we hope they will provide. In loving anyone, however, we take
an interest in *that* person, as a person and not just as a vehicle to
something else. Unless the beloved satisfied needs and desires, we
could not love at all. But love does more than merely duplicate these

interests: it adds a new one, an interest in the object as an autonomous being whose separate importance we now affirm. However much we may go *through* the beloved, as Freud and Santayana suggest, we love him or her as an opaque reality arresting our attention, forcing our imagination to find the appropriate manner of responding to what he or she is.

What Freud misses throughout is the play of imagination in love, and in love's creativity, its ability to bestow a new value apart from any that may be correctly or incorrectly appraised. The idea that happy love depends on massive self-deception Freud inherits from Romantic thinkers who considered love a peculiar way of knowing, remarkably given to erroneous evaluations because it always follows the joyous but unreliable feelings of the heart. For them love is good emotion, whatever its defects as science or metaphysics may be. That part of their belief Freud rejects, but he retains the implausible assumption that love must always be illusory.

For his part, Santayana understands the nature of imagination as well as anyone ever has. Yet he restricts it to an area in which appraisal dominates to the exclusion of creative bestowal. His "ideal object" is something contemplated as a perfection and therefore as a standard against which to test relative excellence. If one were appraising objective value, one might conceivably keep such standards in mind. In a beauty contest the judges *could* reach their decision by comparing each contestant with some ideal type of femininity. They would use imagination both in choosing the ideal and in determining how each woman approaches it. But theirs would not be the loving attitude. For the judges must *not* bestow a special value upon any of the contestants. In principle at least, they must keep their personal feelings in abeyance and remain faithful to the ideal type. By treating his beloved as an end, however, the lover renounces the need to compare her with something else. His love is not a way of ranking her in relation to the ideal. He cares about *her as a par-*

ticular person despite her imperfections, despite her inevitable distance from any or all ideals.

In doing this, the lover uses his imagination not to see an ideal object reflected through another human being but rather to find means of acting as if that person were ideal as he or she actually exists. What does that mean? Not that the beloved impersonates an ideal object, or even reminds the lover of it. It means only that the lover has bestowed incalculable value upon him or her, responding to this individual with great and positive affirmation. The lover's attitude is more than just appraisive. And even in appraisal, Santayana is wrong to think that decisions are made by determining the approximation to an ideal entity. Our standards are rarely that precise. The judges in a beauty contest would be hard put to describe the qualities of the perfect female. And how many lovers could?[12]

In one place Santayana claims that without idealization of *his* sort love would not be love; it would be just "a friendly and humorous affection."[13] That line of reasoning seems untenable. What turns friendly affection into love is not a search for dubious ideal objects but simply a stronger and more extensive bestowal of value. Santayana claims that love concerns itself with possibilities rather than facts. But what are these possibilities? Are they real potentialities of the beloved or just bare essences, self-contained and self-consistent but unrelated to the beloved as he or she is? If the latter, why call it love? The attitude sounds more like a subtle form of aggression against the reality of another person. In the endless realm of possibilities everyone can always be different, and infinitely better than at present. But we do not show our love by imagining these ideal abstractions, except when they reveal what that other person is and actively desires.

I will return to this argument in the following chapter. Here I wanted to establish that possibilities cannot be wholly separated from facts as Santayana believes. His thinking about idealization may teach us how to use persons as a way of loving ideals, but can it show us how to use ideals as a way of loving persons? I think not.

❀

I therefore find Santayana and Freud both deficient as analysts of idealization. Each espouses a different kind of reductivism, based however upon a similar mistake about valuation. But possibly there is another way in which their ideas may be taken. Perhaps we do best to treat them as moralists. Not narrow-minded preachers to be sure, but writers who are *making* ideals in the very process of analyzing them as they issue out of human attitudes.

This is especially evident in Santayana. He advocates an ideal of love and is not only describing it. In characterizing "true love" as he does, he offers criteria for achieving a life worth living through a particular employment of imagination. Defining the word *love* as the search for embodied perfections, he testifies to the goodness in this as opposed to any other way of life. Romantic philosophers had often glorified a love of imperfections and the destructive element, as if appraisal had nothing to do with love, as if all bestowals were equally justifiable. Santayana attacks these beliefs by stressing his own kind of appraisal. As a substitute for nineteenth-century romanticism, he offers a sophisticated Platonistic naturalism that people in the present may very well find inspirational as well as conducive to their needs. This philosophy of love warrants detailed examination.

5 Santayana's Philosophy of Love

THOUGH PROFESSIONAL philosophers in America and elsewhere have returned to Santayana's works in a way that could hardly have been predicted when he died, his thinking about the nature of love has not been adequately studied. In Chapter 4 I discussed shortcomings in his concept of idealization. His ideas are richer than I could indicate there, however, and they require renewed investigation.

Speaking of Santayana as a twentieth-century Platonist, I tried to show how he used his Platonism to oppose the type of materialism that Freud represents. But it would have been equally valid to have started with Santayana's own materialism as the basis of his philosophy. In his speculations on love, scattered through all his books, that is how Santayana usually begins his analysis. I will do likewise. Over and beyond Santayana's materialism and Platonism, I also detect a humanistic voice that differs from both of them. I find Santayana's humanism the most promising element in his approach.

The materialistic strand establishes Santayana as a direct descendent of Schopenhauer. When he was a graduate student, he originally thought of writing his Ph.D. thesis on Schopenhauer's philosophy. He was finally dissuaded by the realization that a sympathetic dissertation of that sort would not provide sufficient opportunity to reveal his own ideas. He also feared that Josiah Royce might not welcome the favorable treatment of naturalistic concepts that Santayana's would be. By the time he wrote *Egotism in German Philosophy,* Santayana had developed a more critical approach to Schopenhauerian pessimism. He found irresolvable difficulties in Schopenhauer's lingering romanticism. Even so, Santayana praises him in that book. He greatly prefers Schopenhauer to "those unspeakable optimists" who thought the troubled world must be good because it makes such a fine tragedy.[1]

What Santayana admires most in Schopenhauer is his insistence on the material grounding of all experience and of all reality. Though what Schopenhauer called the will might occasionally attain spiritual goals, it is not itself spirit. It is just the powerful but purposeless energy in natural process, and therefore the underlying substance in the realm of matter. In Santayana's ontology that realm has the same ultimacy as the deterministic force of destiny which is the will in Schopenhauer. If anything, Santayana is more of a materialist than Schopenhauer. Dismissing Romantic views that portray the will heroically contriving to deny itself through acts of contemplation or proud defiance, Santayana accentuates Schopenhauer's belief that brute and mindless matter is the only substance, that it alone sustains being of any kind.

The implications of Santayana's materialism appear even in his earliest statements about love. In *The Sense of Beauty* (1896) he introduces into a section on "The Materials of Beauty" a discussion about "the influence of the passion of love." Though he is doing aesthetics, he makes remarks that are relevant to the philosophy of love in general. He argues that the sexual instinct needed for purposes of reproduction underlies our perception of beauty in another person as well as our ability to love that particular individual. He tells us that there exists a "machinery" (unspecified but presumably discoverable by empirical science) that directs all animals to their proper object of libidinal desire. He even analyzes "lifelong fidelity to one mate" as a differentiation related to successful reproduction of the species.

But though the sexual instinct cannot be satisfied unless an appropriate object is singled out, Santayana believes that this process operates only with "a great deal of groping and waste." From this there arise the effects, which Santayana considers secondary, of beauty and of love: "For it is precisely from the waste, from the radiation of a sexual passion, that beauty borrows warmth. . . . The capacity to love gives our contemplation that glow without which it might often fail to manifest beauty."[2]

In saying this, Santayana is consciously espousing a reductivistic thesis about love as well as beauty. Like many other materialists and realists, he does so with a sense of admiration, even reverence, for the creative goodness in the sexual drive. He sees it as a "dumb and powerful" faculty that can nevertheless "suffuse the world with the deepest meaning." Unlike traditional moralists, he emphasizes the social and spiritual tendencies that sexual attraction can induce. He reminds us of Stendhal, in one place claiming that "all these new values crystallise about the objects then offered to the mind." He even cites Stendhal's *De l'Amour* after saying that when the new values focus in a single image "the object becomes perfect, and we are said to be in love."[3]

Santayana's reductivism is of a double nature. Not only does he explain love in terms of sexual instinct, but also he derives all love from the relationship between a man and a woman. He says that we become lovers of nature when the values normally crystallized within the image of another person are "dispersed" over the world. And though "woman is the most lovely object to man, and man, if female modesty would confess it, the most interesting to woman," he remarks that repression or frustration often redirect sexual passion toward other ends. These include religion and philanthropy as well as the love of nature. "We may say, then, that for man all nature is a secondary object of sexual passion, and that to this fact the beauty of nature is largely due."[4] In a similar vein Santayana traces back to the needs of the reproductive function virtually all the social dispositions that constitute civilization and social enterprise.

One can only speculate about the degree to which Santayana's thinking was influenced by Freud even at this stage. By 1923, however, the points at which their ideas make contact are prominent in the essay Santayana wrote after he had read *Beyond the Pleasure Principle*. In "A Long Way Round to Nirvana; or Much Ado About Dying," Santayana contrasts Freud's dualistic materialism with Bergson's belief in a "general impulse toward some unknown but single ideal."[5] He recognizes that both conceptions are mythical; but Freud's he finds true to nature, while Bergson's he condemns as folly. Speaking always as a moralist and metaphysician, Santayana perceives in Freud's approach a chastening insight into our condition as material entities. "The transitoriness of things is essential to their physical being, and not at all sad in itself."

What Santayana does find sad is the frustration or destruction of instinctual impulses, arrested before their latent potency has had a chance to express itself and reach fruition. Assuming the rightness of Freud's dictum that "the goal of all life is death," Santayana implies that if all their instincts could be gratified harmoniously human beings would have no further reason to stay alive. In that event, he surmises, "we should be satisfied once and for all and completely. Then doing and dying would coincide throughout and be a perfect pleasure."[6]

Almost twenty years earlier Santayana developed a similar notion in the chapter of *Reason in Society* entitled "Love." Depicting the sexual origins of love in general, he suggests that when passion is vehement and fulfilled it may renounce even life itself, "now that the one fated destiny and all-satisfied good has been achieved." Quoting Siegfried's paean to *Liebestod* at the moment when he and Brünnehilde merge with each other in Wagner's *Ring*, Santayana remarks: "When love is absolute it feels a profound impulse to welcome death, and even, by a transcendental confusion, to invoke the end of the universe."[7]

In the context of his discussion, it is evident that Santayana is not reverting to Romantic metaphysics. For he immediately mentions instincts other than the sexual, instincts related to parenthood. These supervene upon passion and prevent the "transcendental illusion" from causing a total extinction. Instead of death there is the creation of new life, renunciation being followed by a resurrection in the birth of children. By introducing parental instincts of this sort, Santayana remains faithful to his vision as a materialist, for the nature of passionate love is still taken as basically dependent upon the needs of reproduction.

In this vein Santayana praises Lucretius as "the most ingenuous and magnificent of poets," criticizing him only because he described sex in terms of its external behavior and thus neglected the beauty of its inner life—the joy and feverish intensity of libidinal impulse as it is actually experienced by each member of a species. Santayana calls this the "glory of animal love." As a staunch materialist and naturalistic philosopher, he laments the human tendency to consider sexual passion a shame or sin rather than an opportunity for communion through "the most delightful of nature's mysteries." Later in the chapter he refers to "the quality of love" as "its thrill, flutter, and absolute sway over happiness and misery."[8]

To explain how it is possible for the innocent goodness of sex to have been degraded in the course of man's development, Santayana suggests that emotions such as shamefulness result from the relative complexity of human nature. Having a large gamut of instinctual needs, our species is subject to the continuous interaction between sexual desires and other impulses that inhibit sex while also submitting to its pressure. Santayana's brief reference to a field of interacting forces that determine an eventual erotic response is derived from William James's psychology.[9] The idea is important here because it implicitly takes Santayana's conception beyond its reductivistic limits. If shame (or any other attitude related to interpersonal feelings) occurs as a vector of conflicting forces, it cannot be reduced to one of them. And indeed Santayana's approach changes throughout the rest of his chapter. He has less to say about the sexual basis of love than about its function as an imaginative questing for ideals. Santayana's Neoplatonism then becomes the dominant theme in his analysis.

To my knowledge Santayana never calls himself a Neoplatonist, or a Platonist of any kind. In the chapter on love he complains that Plato ignored the "natural history" of the subject. Nevertheless, Santayana repeatedly acknowledges his indebtedness to much of what is most distinctive in Plato's philosophy: the idea that passion, and love as a whole, is elicited by an object that seems good; that this object embodies or represents or symbolizes an ideal goodness and beauty; and that ultimately—in its final definition—love yearns primarily for the ideal itself and not for the imperfect object that happens to prefigure it.

Although he drew upon these elements of Platonic philosophy, Santayana rightly saw that they need not conflict with his underlying naturalism. In *Platonism and the Spiritual Life* he attacks the "Platonic tradition" for having assumed that ideals have any being as substances. He insists that ideals have no existence prior to the occurrence of matter. Throughout his writings, Santayana maintains that only nature or materiality exists as substance. Ideals emerge as goals that organisms create in the process of adapting to their environment. From this it follows that the origins of love are material, even though its aim or objective is the perfection encompassed by an ideal. Synthesizing Platonism with naturalism in this way, Santayana believes that "every ideal expresses some natural function, and that no natural function is incapable, in its free exercise, of evolving some ideal. . . . For love is a brilliant illustration of a principle everywhere discoverable: namely, that human interest lives by turning the friction of material forces into the light of ideal goods."[10]

Both early and late, Santayana frequently describes love as a "sublimation" related to an "animal basis," and to this extent his kinship to Freud remains intact.[11] But Plato too had thought that love begins in each person's history as a physical, indeed sexual, phenomenon, although it manifests a fundamental longing for possession of a transcendental good. In Plato's writings, however, we constantly encounter a systematic ambiguity about natural and ideal love. Must material interests be eliminated, or cleansed, in order for the lover to carry out the metaphysical mission? Is love a harmonious completion of organic needs, such as the sexual, or is it rather a oneness with the principle of goodness and beauty which necessitates quasi-ascetic contemplation?

By insisting upon the interrelation between ideals and natural processes, Santayana continues the effort of Neoplatonists in the Renaissance who tried to resolve Plato's ambiguities. Like Ficino, Santayana sees love as a search for ideals that appear in the midst of nature, and as an inherent part of nature. Ficino, like other Platonistic Christians, thought that ideals emanate from a super-world beyond nature. Santayana parts company at this juncture, but he never deviates from the belief that love constitutes a transmuting of natural desires into a pursuit of ideals that direct us toward the putative goodness in everything that is desired.

If this were all that Santayana said about love, one might be tempted to dismiss him as a naturalist who weaves a minimal bit of Neoplatonism into the fabric of his thought. Apart from its belletristic beauties, the chapter on love in *Reason in Society* is remarkable only in its repeated claim that ideals such as married love or the love of humanity may be explained as sublimations of sexual desire. But even in 1905, when the book was published, this suggestion was hardly novel. Santayana's development of his Platonistic insights, in later books, is what reveals the great originality in his synthesis. The major text is *The Realm of Spirit,* the final volume of *Realms of Being.* It was published in 1940, at a bad moment in the history of the Western world, and it has never received the attention it deserves. In it Santayana's thinking about love reaches a height beyond anything he had previously attained.

Regardless of the connotations that the term *spirit* often has, Santayana's conception is thoroughly naturalistic. Like everything else that exists, spirit belongs to processes in the material world; it arises from the realm of matter. Spirit has no substantial being in itself. As the sole substance, matter creates spirit after developing into a special form of life, the disposition of vital energy which is psyche. "The self-maintaining and reproducing pattern or structure of an organism, conceived as a power, is called a psyche."[12]

When psyches become active in their relations to the physical world, Santayana tells us, they achieve an animal as well as a vegetative condition. If spirit then awakens in animals, it does so as a kind of "moral illumination" or "free entertainment." In his glossary of terms, Santayana defines spirit as "an awareness natural to animals, revealing the world and themselves in it. Other names for spirit are consciousness, attention, feeling, thought, or any word that marks the total *inner* difference between being awake or asleep, alive or dead." Elsewhere he says: "Spirit is only that inner light of actuality or attention which floods all life as men actually live it on earth." And later, when he discusses the sense in which there may be freedom in spirit, he remarks that spirit is "the invisible but immediate fact that matter with its tropes and powers is being observed, conceived, enjoyed, asserted, or desired: a vitality essentially moral, invisible, and private, absolutely actual and thoroughly unsubstantial, always self-existent and totally vanishing as it lives."[13]

By formulating this concept of spirit, Santayana discards all supernatural ideas about a soul or spiritual entity that could exist apart from the material world. He also rejects idealistic notions about spirit as a supreme power that determines the direction of the universe, whether by creating it in advance or by animating its progressive evolution. On the contrary, Santayana maintains that spirit—as opposed to psyche, which is a biological agency of material being—always remains impotent, wholly ineffectual, capable of surveying the universe but unable to alter it. Changes in the order of things may result from psyche working upon the world as a functionary within animal activity. Spirit is one of these changes.

Its existence depends on the interrelation between psyche and the natural environment. But in spirit itself there can be "nothing persistent or potential. It is pure light and perpetual actuality."[14]

If we now ask what it is that spirit illuminates in its actuality and purified light, Santayana replies in terms of his ideas about essences. Being the character or whatness of everything given to consciousness, these result either directly from intuition, or analytically from dialectical reasoning, or symbolically from imagination. Santayana's doctrine of essences resembles the Platonic theory of forms inasmuch as both assume that man has the capacity to contemplate the world in its immediacy and without necessarily interpreting it as something that exists. Far from being an insight into a vital impulse that is foundational to all existence—as Bergson would say—awareness of essence is for Santayana an aptitude of the mind which lights upon the pattern and apparent quality of everything that is merely possible, whether or not it has existed or ever will exist.

Santayana's essences are nothing but pure possibilities. In thinking of anything that is not self-contradictory, we entertain a quality without which nothing could even be conceived—its inherent form, its defining attributes. Everything that is not logically incompatible or incoherent will be a possible in this sense. That is why we can have reveries about unicorns and golden mountains although we know that no such entities will come into existence. There can be no essence of a round square, for that yokes together wholly inconsistent terms and hence provides no viable possibility for the mind to contemplate. Since everything that exists must also be possible, we have access to the realm of matter through the realm of essence. But Santayana insists upon the ontological difference between these realms, as Plato also does, because he wishes to call our attention to the implications of living in accordance with one or the other mode of approaching reality.

In Plato's philosophy, as it is usually interpreted, the doctrine of forms is designed to show how mankind can obtain certain knowledge through its use of a priori reason. Santayana offers no such prospect. He is a skeptic in epistemology, and he argues that what counts as knowledge is inevitably based on the mythological feeling he calls animal faith. Moreover, Plato considered the forms to be hierarchically ordered in the sense that those providing greater levels of generality are more reliable for the acquisition of truth than the ones that pertain to data from our bodily senses. On the highest level stood the Good or the Beautiful, since everything is purposively geared toward the achievement of ultimate values present in the universe as infinite and eternal possibilities. Little of this idealism survives in Santayana's conception. For him all essences are alike in being the content of a clarified intuition, and therefore each is a comparable revelation of possible reality as we experience it.

As I have suggested, Plato's doctrine is the one that judges of a dog show might use in their attempt to find the perfect collie or basset hound. But Santayana insists that in principle every competitor, whatever its attributes, is a suitable exemplar of some possibility that defines its being and serves as an appropriate essence for us to idealize. Just as he affords no causal or teleological efficacy to the realm of forms, neither does Santayana accept the Platonic assumption that the universe is innately and objectively structured in accordance with any hierarchical ordering of essences.

Even so, Santayana does retain Plato's belief in the value and importance of the contemplative attitude. Focusing its light on the being of whatever object, spirit longs for the potential goodness in everything. Because it is only a fortuitous emanation of psyche, spirit cannot change the world. But having intuited essences, it seeks for what it defines as beautiful in them. This depends on imagination, and Santayana remarks that "the only possible way for spirit to create is to imagine."[15]

In saying this, Santayana sounds more like a nineteenth-century

Romantic than like a Platonist. His Platonism shows itself, however, when he portrays spirit's attachment to mere potentialities as opposed to anything that exists or can be physically possessed. In the first of the epigraphs that precede *The Realm of Spirit,* Santayana quotes from a passage in which Plotinus, speaking of love, says, "This spirit is generated out of the psyche in the measure in which she lacks the good, yet yearns after it."[16] Such a view of love and of spirit is wholly coherent with what Santayana stated in *Reason in Society* about the "ideality" of love. He there argued that, in its purified and sublimated condition, love transcends the material world and "yearns for the universe of values." Despite its origins in matter—that is, reproductive necessity—love's "true object is no natural being, but an ideal form essentially eternal and capable of endless embodiments."[17]

In *Reason in Society* these statements about the ideality of love adumbrate much of what Santayana later developed in his mature ontology. By the time that *The Realm of Spirit* was written, however, he had become sensitive to the contradictions within spirit itself. It was not only a light that shines upon the actuality of what is given or the possible qualities of what can be imagined, but it also included a painful recognition of its inability to make the world better. Santayana now saw spirit as a disposition rent by two different kinds of love. Spirit, he finally concluded, "is inwardly divided and confused."[18]

Since it is a product of "universal Will," capitalized as if in recognition of Schopenhauer's German usage, Santayana declares that spirit must love the love in everything. It must feel sympathy for all the forms that life may take and for all the ideal fulfillments that are possible to living things in their diverse cravings. But the will in one organism competes with that of another, and each occasion of spirit occurs within a psyche that seeks its personal welfare. However much spirit may wish to identify with every search for goodness, it is hampered by the selfish demands of its governing psyche and by the limitations that this imposes upon its capacity for dispassionate love. As Santayana says: "Will here must sympathize with all Will and must love with all lovers; yet it must condemn each Will, not for loving that which it loves but for not loving that which it does not love; in other words, for not loving the good in all its possible forms. But all goods cannot be realized or sanely pursued in any particular life. Only the specific goals of that place and hour are proper to that particular concretion of universal Will."[19]

Articulating this contradiction within spirit, Santayana detects an inevitable conflict between existence and what he calls justice. Being an offshoot of matter in one or another configuration, spirit arises as an aspiration toward particular goals. But in itself, in accordance with its essence, it sympathizes with all potential exemplifications of goodness or beauty, wherever and however they may occur. Santayana calls this "the most tragic of conflicts."[20] He claims that there is no way in which it can be avoided. On the contrary, he insists that spirit fulfills its nature by accepting its inability to eliminate the conflict, by submitting to its own impotence in the world, and in that sense choosing renunciation as its fate.

When it makes this choice, spirit does not escape suffering. But it learns how to benefit from it. In its allegiance to "intelligence, sympathy, universality," spirit acquiesces in the fact that it must suffer and thereby purifies its own spirituality. For spirit does more than just intuit ideals that reveal possible goods within the universe. It also hungers to become purified in itself. Herein consists another contradiction that Santayana exploits. Writing specifically about spirit in relation to love, he describes the latter as a vital attachment without which the former could not exist. Love "experiences a physical affinity between the psyche and the object."[21] To that extent, it precedes spirit rather than depending on it.

Nevertheless, as Santayana also maintains, love subsumes its object under the aspect of an ideal goodness, thus clothing it "in spiritual guise."[22] Through the dynamics of love, each vital attachment progresses into a striving for inner purity that defines the realm of spirit. This realm is not another world; it is not an example of "cosmic animism" or any other metaphysical dimension beyond the actuality of ordinary life. In its purity spirit aspires toward the same perfection that love seeks once it sublimates its instinctual or possessive needs into a detached appreciation that renounces the world in the very process of accepting it.

One can make various criticisms of Santayana's view. As I have remarked, the concept of idealization that he employs prevents one from understanding the love of persons. If love defines itself as perceiving its object under the aspect of an ideal beauty or goodness that this individual symbolizes and even represents, it is the ideal that is really loved rather than the object. In that event we are in love with a possible perfection and not with the man or woman as a person. When Santayana says that in love the true object is not a natural being but an ideal form "essentially eternal and capable of endless embodiments," he depicts love as *just* an idealization. How then can one love another as the particularity that he or she happens to be?[23]

This difficulty applies to Santayana's later writings as well as to his earlier ones, to *The Realm of Spirit* as well as to *Reason in Society*. In terms of his final ideas about spirit, the dilemma appears within the paradox I previously discussed. As jointly the products of psyche, both love and spirit result from desire for a specific good embodied in an object. Spirit refines love, and possibly issues into its own kind of love, by detaching the organism from mere possessiveness and shining the light of adoration upon a universal potentiality for goodness. This means that love has two types of essences, two modalities or levels of being. In one it operates within the realm of matter. In the other it reaches for a spiritual love that surmounts any vital attachment to a single object while also accepting it as the approximation of an ideal.

The first of these is a love of things, and it may possibly account for the erotic bonding that instinctually causes us to seek one or another kind of sexual pleasure. The second love that Santayana defines is closer to a love of ideals. Though arising from human aspirations, ideals enable us to move beyond any momentary or local state in which we happen to exist.[24] Both are authentic types of love, and in his great sensitivity to the role that imagination plays in each, Santayana brilliantly portrays their complex relation to each other.

What Santayana does not understand, or recognize fully, is the fact that a love of persons cannot be explained as either a love of things or a love of ideals, whether they occur individually or in conjunction with each other. Interpersonal love involves more than possessiveness or renunciation. It is neither instinctual gratification of a wholly material sort nor the sacrificial martyrdom of one's own interests, and neither a blind yearning for domination nor a willed and willing detachment that culminates in contemplation at a distance. The love of persons endures by being what it was in its origins—a vital attachment. But in being love directed toward others in themselves, as persons, it is also a bestowing of values that may create a unique and sometimes beneficial oneness that Santayana's perspective can scarcely accommodate.

If my criticism is justified, one must conclude that Santayana's synthesis has not succeeded. Matter and spirit have been interpreted in a way that does not elucidate what is most in need of explanation. That is part of what William James meant when he called Santayana's philosophy a perfection of rottenness. He did not wish to malign Santayana or to deny his competence as a philosopher. He was not saying that Santayana's philosophy was perfectly rotten. He was referring to Santayana's combination of Platonism and materialism, which James considered faulty. And if Santayana's vision of the world includes only the superimposition of possible perfections on the rottenness that belongs to its material substance, is he not ignoring the ability of human beings to live a good though imperfect life within a natural condition that is neither completely bad nor entirely destructive?[25]

Santayana offered his analysis as a means of remaining absolutely faithful to the reality he knew. His was a tragic view of life precisely because he saw no grounds for minimizing basic differences between the realms of matter and of spirit. What justification could there be in putting on a brave show of confidence, as he thought that James pervasively did, instead of admitting the fearful truths of our ontology and learning how to cope with them? Santayana's courage is undeniable. And yet the structure of his philosophy— in contrast to his creativity in writing it—fails to show us how people can overcome the split between matter and spirit. In misrepresenting the love of persons, he neglects a major segment of human nature that cuts across these ontological categories.

The crack in Santayana's golden bowl recurs in all his statements about love. As in Platonism throughout the centuries, his conception repeatedly introduces a note of sadness and despair. Human beings strive for ideals that lift the heart and invigorate the spirit but eternally elude our grasp because we are creatures forever bound by an alien materiality. Santayana's epigram about Platonic love is indicative: "All beauties attract by suggesting the ideal and then fail to satisfy by not fulfilling it."[26] There is an aura of frustration and depression that surrounds these words. Though they express a view of the world that has inspired much of the greatest poetry, and though they reflect the disappointments that are always possible in love despite the grandeur of its quest, they also reek of subjective failure arbitrarily projected upon the facts of life. Whatever Santayana's sexuality may have been, his outlook belongs to the experience of those who are not secure within their erotic orientation and do not live in a society that allows them to value and attain their own type of personal development.

Within Santayana's writings we occasionally find him referring to deviant behavior in language that is quite negative though somewhat veiled. Like Ficino and other Neoplatonists, and like Plato in the *Laws,* he speaks of homosexuality as depraved and possibly diseased. On the other hand, there is little reason to believe that he himself savored the varied delights of heterosexual love. All beauties—male and female—may well have attracted him, but could any eliminate the painful inhibitions with which he was reared?

I do not wish to magnify the relevance of these biographical details. I mention them only to highlight Santayana's assertion that "a perfect love is founded on despair. . . . The *perfect* lover must renounce pursuit and the hope of possession."[27] In another work he amplifies this view by saying that "possession leaves the true lover unsatisfied: his joy is in the character of the thing loved, in the essence it reveals."[28] The first part of this sentence is reminiscent of Proust's statement that in sexual possession we possess nothing (and therefore we remain unsatisfied); the second part sounds like Proust using Platonistic language to express his own idea of essences. Regardless of the philosophical differences between Proust and Santayana, they both write as men who were disqualified from appreciating the possibilities of a satisfying sexual love for any other person. Santayana could be speaking for Proust when he asserts that "contemplation is the whole object of love, and the sole gain in loving."[29]

Santayana was aware that contemplation can be problematic. In an essay on "Plotinus and the Nature of Evil," he says: "I know that in practice a devotion that passes from individuals to the ideal is . . . commonly only a sort of abstract sensuality or aestheticism, at once selfish and visionary." Nevertheless, Santayana is convinced that the "genuine Platonist" solves such difficulties by loving individuals so intensely that they become "the revelation of an essence greater than theirs, of something that, could we live always in its presence, would render us supremely happy."[30] Still he remarks elsewhere that when we recognize the imperfection of the individual object "love turns into suffering." He even wonders: "If ever we have ceased to suffer, have we not ceased to love?"[31]

Since contemplation (as Santayana interprets it) affects the experience of love in this way, we can understand why he claims: "It is not persons, in their personal limitations, that can enter into a spiritual union."[32] Santayana likens this "union of spirits" to the relationship between souls as Dante portrays them in the *Paradiso*. "Persons become translucent," he states, but he does little to clarify what this can possibly mean. He probably has in mind a circumstance in which people perceive one another as just the essences they show forth.

Although Santayana describes this union of translucent spirits as different from the interpersonal love between men or women who *accept* each other as they are, he does suggest that "contact or friendship" between persons can have an important role in the emergence of spirituality.[33] Because spirit cannot occur without psyche, he points out, it requires a healthy affiliation between persons as a preliminary to the transcending of its origins. A successful love of persons might thus provide a springboard for spiritual attainments. But Santayana does not believe that spirituality and the love of persons are similar in their defining properties. According to him, the love of persons achieves its ideality only as it is sublimated, and therefore submerged, in the service of spirituality.

Santayana's doubts about the love of persons appear most clearly in a chapter entitled "Distraction." He begins by claiming that "frank love," by which he means lovemaking directed toward immediate pleasures of the senses, is not an impediment to spirit. In itself the flesh does not cause distractions, particularly when "love turns the flesh into loveliness." Far from being threatened by an appetite for sexual goods, which Santayana deems innocent in themselves, spirit can readily arise as a purification of one's passion. This happens when love "ceases to be a craving for the unknown. . . . The object then proves to have been an essence and not an existing person or thing; and among essences there is no jealousy or contradiction, and no decay."[34]

Distraction occurs when spirit becomes enmeshed in attachments to things or persons that may create "domestic virtue" but scarcely spiritual freedom. "In marriage," Santayana maintains, "love is socialized and moralized into a lifelong partnership which it would be dishonourable to betray; and community of interests and habits buttresses that love into mutual trust and assistance."[35] But in the very next sentence, he adds: "A household rather smothers the love that established it."

How then can spirit escape the distractions of the world? How can it liberate itself from the duties and responsibilities that it knows to be morally defensible though inevitably a confining of its free exercise? As always, Santayana's answer presupposes the need to transform personal involvement into contemplative sublimation. To avoid distraction, spirit "will distinguish the loveliness in things or the charm in persons from the existing persons and things. These were the vehicle, *that* was the revelation." What he calls "the straight-jacket imposed by society" seemed less pernicious to Santayana than "the illusions, revulsions, suspicions, and disasters suffered by love itself when given a free rein." Santayana calls these possible occurrences the "vital contradictions" of love.[36] He scarcely intimates that the love of persons can include a system of values not at all inimical to spirit.

In Santayana's defense one might argue that the condition he explicates is a *purity* of spirit that must not be reduced even to the love between persons. When Santayana talks about "pure spirit" or "the spiritual life," he should be taken as referring to a possible achievement—an excellence in spirit, a kind of superior subdivision within the realm of spirit. While depicting spirit as the actuality of mind when it attends to what is given or is possible (in other words, when it merely contemplates or imagines), Santayana defines *spirituality* as spirit trying to exclude everything but itself. Though the spiritual life, like spirit in general, is an outgrowth of psyche and the realm of matter, it seeks to disintoxicate itself from them.

The word *disintoxicate* often occurs in Santayana's writings, as if to suggest that spirit becomes sober and pellucid only when it treats its material origins as if they were foreign to its being. Santayana does believe that pure spirit will recognize the goodness of all earthly loves: having disintoxicated itself, it will perceive the beauty that is in them. But it will not love anything as the world does. For it will not concern itself with existence focused in a particular object, whether a person or a thing, and it will avoid all bonds that impair its own purified kind of love.

In *Platonism and the Spiritual Life,* where Santayana discusses spirituality as a path anyone may follow, he holds that it exceeds even Plato's philosophy of love. That still involves a search for goodness, for values that a life of spirit transcends just as they themselves transcend materiality. The greatest literary expression of spirituality he finds, not in the philosophic texts of Greece, but in the religious documents of India.

Closer to his own origins, Santayana uses his ideas about spirit to make sense out of Catholicism and Christianity as a whole. In *The Idea of Christ in the Gospels* he analyzes the Christian notion of God in man as a mythic representation of pure spirit providing the only means to salvation. Embodying the principles of renunciation, detachment, liberation from the world, but also appreciation of its underlying universal goodness, Christ is seen as an idealization of the suffering human spirit that triumphantly disintoxicates itself from the lures and miseries of existence.

To the end of his life Santayana remained a "Catholic atheist," as he has been called.[37] He never wavered in his adherence to materialism, but his delineation of—and obvious admiration for— the spiritual life reveals the depths of his permanent allegiance to Catholicism.

In view of this, we may wonder why Santayana asserts that he is closer to the Greeks than to the Indians, and that he aspires to a life of rationality rather than spirituality. The former inclination suggests a quest for harmony among interests, whereas the latter calls for a single-minded pursuit that casts aside everything but itself. Do we have to choose between these alternatives? That is the question that Santayana examines dialectically in one of the chapters of his *Dialogues in Limbo*. In the dialogue entitled "The Philanthropist," Socrates and The Stranger converse about two ways in which mankind can be loved. In effect, one is love coherent with the life of reason and the other is love that issues from pure spirituality.

In describing both possibilities, Santayana voices aspects of his own philosophy that could easily appear to contradict each other. On the one hand, we are presented with a conception of humanistic "philanthropy," which Socrates defends. In opposition to this idea, The Stranger argues for what he calls charity. Philanthropy is a love of mankind which Socrates considers essentially "the love of an idea, and not of actual men and women." Philanthropy directs itself toward what is truly good for human beings; it is geared to the realities of their nature and aims for a "perfect humanity" that ideally would provide fulfillment, regardless of what some individual may happen to desire. The Stranger claims that "any adoration of mankind is mere sentimentality, killed by contact with actual men and women. Towards actual people a doting love signifies silliness in the lover and injury to the beloved, until that love is chastened into charity." Santayana employs the word *charity* in approximation of the medieval concept of caritas and not as the word is more commonly used nowadays. He thinks charity is godlike even if it exists only in human beings. The Stranger calls it "a sober and profound compassion . . . succouring distress everywhere and helping all to endure their humanity and to renounce it."[38]

In this notion of charity we may recognize the disposition that Santayana generally assigns to pure spirit. Transcending the search for perfection and aspiring toward emancipation from the world, the spiritual life is an exclusive commitment to charity. The Stranger remarks that charity "is less than philanthropy in that it expects the defeat of man's natural desires and accepts that defeat; and it is more than philanthropy in that, in the face of defeat, it brings consolation." Socrates sums up the discussion with the suggestion that "philanthropy is a sentiment proper to man in view of his desired perfection, and charity a sentiment proper to a god, or to a man inspired by a god, in view of the necessary imperfection of all living creatures."[39]

Santayana leaves the dialogue with this minimal synthesis between the two ideals. Though charity is a Christian concept, he makes little attempt to defend Christianity itself. The Stranger classifies that religion as one among other "domesticated evils or tonic poisons, like the army, the government, the family, and the school; all of them traditional crutches, with which, though limping, we manage to walk."[40] Even this halfhearted recommendation seems overly generous to Socrates, who gives thanks that he died before the Christian era. At the same time, we must realize that the dialectical play between the voices of Socrates and The Stranger duplicates the ambivalence in Christianity between its indigenous concepts of eros and agapē. In *The Realm of Spirit,* in a passage subtitled "Charity *versus* Eros," Santayana discusses the theological controversy about love that descends regardless of what the object merits as distinct from love that seeks to attain perfection. In different contexts he offers varying solutions to the problem.

At times Santayana insists that, properly speaking, all love must be subsumed under the concept of eros. For love issues from the psyche and can only desire something that will ideally satisfy it: "There is therefore no love not directed upon . . . something that makes for the fulfillment of the lover's nature. This good may be the good of others, but doing good to others will to that extent be a good for oneself."[41] It would follow from this that perfect charity is not really love, and Santayana does argue that orthodox beliefs about God being love are therefore hardly coherent within themselves. In *Platonism and the Spiritual Life* he likewise asks whether charity is really love since, in its spirituality, it cannot seek perfection as its goal. Santayana nevertheless ends this book with the idea that charity expresses a kind of spiritual love that is not correctly understood by the Platonic approach or by the eros tradition as a whole: "When the renunciation of the world, and of existence itself, has been hearty and radical, the love of nature can be universal;

I will not say unqualified by sadness, because the spirit, having itself suffered, recognizes in many an alien form of existence a maimed effort and a lost glory analogous to its own; but a love unqualified by prejudice, by envy, by fear of being outshone or discountenanced by the marvels which nature or society may elsewhere bring to light. It is of the essence of spirit to see and love things for their own sake, in their own nature, not for the sake of one another, nor for its own sake."[42]

A passage of this sort must give us pause, for it seems to contradict what Santayana says in other places. Still, it would be futile in itself, and harmful for an understanding of Santayana's thought, if we were to charge him with inconsistency in his use of the word *love*. Through its detached compassion and sympathetic concern for the suffering in all existence, charity (as he defines it) involves a loving attitude whether or not it is the type of love that either Santayana or Plato considers best for human beings. At least in part, the love that is charity finds everything worthy of our compassion merely because all things suffer in their joint bondage to the wheel of karma. While renouncing the goods it does not hope to garner for itself, spirit extends its charity to all reality. In his own way, Santayana could be seen as reverting to Nietzsche's notion of *amor fati*.[43]

In *Egotism in German Philosophy*, published in 1915, Santayana condemned Nietzsche for romanticizing evil, for encouraging us to accept it in order to feel the intensity of our own aggressive nature. Santayana shows no desire, throughout his writing, to acquiesce in any doctrine that deifies the exercise of power, even if that leads to happiness for oneself or others. He resembles Nietzsche, however, not only in basing his moral philosophy on naturalistic premises but also in depicting a state in which the human spirit may finally reconcile itself to the evils that attend the frailty and fragility of the world.

Reading from the other direction, we may even find in Nietzsche's doctrine of amor fati an anticipation of Santayana's idea that spirit can liberate itself only by accepting reality through acts of renunciation and self-purification. This is the side of Nietzsche that links him to Schopenhauer. The Nietzschean concept implies something more strenuous, more activistic than the kind of contemplation that Santayana identifies with the spiritual life. But before he returns to the everyday world, Nietzsche's superman withdraws from it, like Zarathustra on the mountain, and to this extent he is purifying the spirit within himself.

All the same, it would be a mistake to confuse Santayana's prime inspiration with either Nietzsche's or Schopenhauer's. In his attempt to create a twentieth-century synthesis between Platonism and materialism, Santayana moves further from romanticism than does either of these German philosophers. His literary criticism abounds with scornful comments about the "barbarism" of such writers as Whitman, Browning, even Goethe, and in general all Romantics who treat the human spirit as anything more than a lonely wanderer in a universe devoid of any basic interest in our welfare.

Santayana's anti-Romantic stance is evident in his assertion that spirit attends to the known rather than some cosmic unknown. This idea appears most fully in his discussion of union in *The Realm of Spirit*. Because substance is always material, and in living creatures individualized in one or another organism, Santayana states that "fusion with the universe is not union but death." The Good toward which spirit may direct itself is a knowable harmony among natural desires. When spirits achieve an attainment of this type, Santayana says, the moral union they establish consists in "perfect unanimity" among themselves. Far from fusing with each other or with the unknown, they jointly affirm the ideal possibilities that the highest moral principle entails for everyone as an individual.[44]

Santayana recognizes no possibility of union apart from the fact that spirits may happen to pursue the same ideals and realize that others can cooperate in an extraneous fashion. "In seeking union with any other spirit," Santayana argues, "we are therefore seeking either the Good, in that this other spirit realizes the perfection to which we are inwardly addressed; or else we are seeking such conformity with power and with truth as is necessary to the attainment of our proper good."[45]

From this it follows that if spirit can ever find complete and authentic union such oneness must be a harmonious attunement within a single spirit. That is in fact what Santayana does believe. He ends the discussion with a vision of spirit free and wholly unified within a concentrated, detached, but also compassionate human being who sympathizes with the yearning for goodness in every thing and every person, though he can never merge with them. Nor does Santayana see any reason to expect permanence or constant perfection in the purified spirit. Like Proust, he tells us that "Intermittence is intrinsic to life, to feeling, to thought; so are partiality and finitude."[46]

In a passage that reminds us of Spinoza as well as the Christian mystics, Santayana's concluding remarks about union describe a victory for spirit embracing in a final restoration the world it has renounced. Having attained unity in its own contemplative nature, spirit enjoys the essential—though not the existential—being of everything. That happens through "intellectual worship, in which spirit, forgetting itself, becomes pure vision and pure love."[47]

❋

In presenting these reflections, Santayana touches upon spiritual possibilities that other materialists have always considered fatuous or bogus. But neither will Santayana's conception satisfy idealists who believe in a separate spirit world from which human beings originate, with which they may commune in this life, and to which they can return after death.

Of greatest import from my perspective, Santayana's ideas about spirit may now be seen as the source of his misconceptions about the love between persons. As long as he treats the spiritual life as the transcending of particularities, he cannot explain how spirit may experience a love that responds to someone else as just the person he or she is, existing in time and space as a conglomeration of specific properties and dispositions. On Santayana's view, pure spirit can never reach the inner core of other spirits or truly interact with them in their actual totality. How else should we interpret his assertions about detachment, renunciation, and acquiescence in the irremedial impotence of spirit? What he describes may be compatible with some forms of sympathy, even compassion, but it scarcely defines interpersonal love.

Nonetheless, we may find Santayana's outlook helpful if we wish to emancipate ourselves from possessiveness, egoism, self-deception, and the restless hunger for dubious goods that makes it impossible for any other kind of attitude to occur. Santayana shows us how pure spirit can obtain joyful serenity by accepting what is given and contemplating what is true or imaginable. This is a form of satori that need not prevent an individual from returning to the world and living in it as an organism capable of satisfying all its faculties. Indeed, the ideal of happiness as the total fulfillment of natural impulses is defended in much of what Santayana wrote, especially in his earlier work. The importance of undertaking practical activities, the philosopher descending from his contemplative state and participating in the wretched world, he does not emphasize as much as Nietzsche or even Plato. But he leaves that open as a viable project that can sometimes fill periods of spiritual intermittence with opportunities for moral conduct. The purified spirit would then be joining forces with the psyche from which it arose, the two combining harmoniously and seeking unification with the desires of other spirits.

In Santayana's later philosophy these intimations of beneficent harmony are left mainly undeveloped. They are compatible, however, with his former writings about the life of reason. As we have seen, he himself denied that there was any significant inconsistency between the two stages in his thought. He explained the differences between them in terms of new ideas that preoccupied him as he got older. Santayana was right about this: he understood the nature of his philosophical development better than the critics who thought he was rejecting reason in favor of spirituality. Although *Realms of Being* calls itself ontology, it reflects Santayana's enlarged experience of life in his later years. That was inevitably different from his experience as a younger man, but he did not proffer an alternative system of analysis that contradicts his earlier philosophy.

In this connection Santayana's comments about friendship, scattered throughout his works, are extremely pertinent. They represent the humanistic strand that always accompanies, and enriches, his writings about either the life of reason or the life of spirit. In *Soliloquies in England* he suggests that "one's friends are that part of the human race with which one can be human." The kind of friendship that mainly interests Santayana is the "union of one whole man with another whole man," which he interprets as "the felt harmony of life with life, and of life with nature."[48]

In this passage, does the word *man* refer to both sexes? Seventeen years before, in a chapter on "Free Society," Santayana maintained that "friends are generally of the same sex, for when men and women agree, it is only in their conclusions; their reasons are always different." A few pages later, however, he tells us that in contemporary society "a well-assorted marriage" approximates, indeed "most nearly resembles," the ancient ideal of friendship that he wants to further. The lines are worth quoting: "In spite of intellectual disparity and of divergence in occupation, man and wife are bound together by a common dwelling, common friends, common affection for children, and, what is of great importance, common financial interests. These bonds often suffice for substantial and lasting unanimity, even when no ideal passion preceded; so that what is called a marriage of reason, if it is truly reasonable, may give a fair promise of happiness, since a normal married life can produce the sympathies it requires."[49]

This declaration reinforces my belief that Santayana does not give us an adequate analysis of the love of persons. The statement reveals that his approach to married love mainly concerns itself with the coordinates of a suitable partnership. The "marriage of reason" that Santayana advocates is the same as the social arrangement Schopenhauer contrasted with the bond of sexual love. Schopenhauer despaired of uniting them within a marital relation, and Santayana makes no attempt to suggest how that might happen. On the other hand, one could argue that Santayana's reference to sympathetic and lasting unanimity does take us part of the way toward understanding how marriage can become a manifestation of heterosexual friendship.

The humanistic (and pluralistic) aspect of Santayana's philosophy of love appears most prominently in his posthumous essay entitled "Friendship." In it he sketches a spectrum of affective values, friendship and charity being the two that intrigue him most, though they are not the only ones he wishes to defend. He contrasts friendship with brotherly or sisterly love, for these depend on family origin rather than free choice. Friendship is "distinctly selective, personal, and exclusive: in this respect it resembles the passion of love." But friendship differs from passionate love, Santayana maintains, in directing imagination outward, toward the world as a whole, rather than focusing it on the relation between the lovers themselves. "What fills the imagination of friends is the world, as a scene for action and an object of judgement; and the person of the friend is distinguished and selected from all others because of exceptionally acceptable ways of acting, thinking, and feeling about other things or other persons." Santayana concludes that friendship is "the union of two freely ranging souls that meet by chance, recognize and prize each other, but remain free."[50]

By citing freedom as fundamental in it, Santayana sets friendship apart from other kinds of love that he discusses. He sees it as bound neither by instincts that serve reproductive necessities nor by social constraints and moral obligations, as in marriage. Yet he insists that friendship is just as "vital and biological" as sexual or marital love. He also distinguishes between friendship and companionship fashioned by business or external circumstances in which "the persons are indifferent, transparent, and exchangeable. . . . In friendship, as in love, the play must have the persons for its authors."[51]

This way of talking about friendship, and about love, is very remote from Santayana's usual variations on either Platonism or materialism. His emphasis upon persons, and the suggestion that they may have importance in themselves, takes him beyond his belief that individuals are merely the vehicle to some cherished ideal. But Santayana's philosophy is incomplete at this point. Though he considers love and friendship similar in their striving for "a vital personal sympathy," he does not describe, or even acknowledge, the ways in which the two may coalesce. He treats sexual and marital love as sentiments controlled by the needs of domesticity, and he seems to take it for granted that the burdens they involve—to say nothing of "jealousy, masterfulness, the desire to monopolise"—must be inimical to friendship. Predicated upon a free choice, and manifesting freedom throughout its career, the friendship he has in mind must belong entirely to the life of spirit. As he has little conception of how spiritual and nonspiritual love may interpenetrate, so too does Santayana ignore the possibility of a love between persons that is sexual or marital and *also* a type of friendship. The rift within his philosophy has not been overcome.

In calling friendship a "union of souls," Santayana might seem to be undermining his claim that spirits cannot fuse with each other. As a matter of fact, his thinking is consistent in this regard. Although he asserts that the union in friendship is "more than agreement," he also refers to it as "a coincidence of free souls."[52] This does not contradict what he says elsewhere about union.

Moreover, his statements about friendship serve as a corrective to the charge that Santayana's later philosophy seeks to orient preferred human relations toward the achievement of spiritual purity. He insists upon the differences between charity and friendship. "Charity, not being intrinsic either to love or to friendship, requires the intervention of imaginative reason, by which we detach ourselves from our accidental persons and circumstances and feel the equal reality of all other persons in all other plights."[53] Santayana extols the infinite beauty in charity, but he affirms that love or friendship or philanthropy can also be beautiful. Nowhere does he suggest that anyone must extirpate natural virtues or devote himself to the peculiar and exclusive interests of pure spirit. That remains a matter of individual choice.

This pluralistic substratum is what I particularly value in Santayana's moral philosophy. It is the portion of his vision from which we can learn the most. In a letter he wrote to a young admirer, Richard C. Lyon, who then became a Santayana scholar, he reformulates the disparate elements in his philosophy of love. If he does not entirely succeed in this attempt, as I still believe, he nevertheless encourages us to find our own solution. The following from his letter makes a suitable ending to this chapter:

Love, in English, is a very wide term. What poets and philosophers, at least of the classic school, talk about is the *passion* of love, the madness, divine madness, of Plato. But attraction, confidence, mutual delight, and complete devotion to a chosen mate is not madness at all, it is a phase, a settlement, of the *sane* affections of one human being to another, where all sane possible bonds, physical, domestic, social, intellectual, and religious bind the two together for life—common material interests and children being strong material buttresses to such a complete union in after years. More than once, at friends' houses in England, or in hotels, I have found myself divided only by a frail closed door from the bed in which an elderly pair were exchanging confidential judgments and ideas; and I have been impressed by the *perfection* of friendship and sympathy in such a union. The only advantage—for me important—that the ideal friendship has over such a happy wedlock is liberty. Friends need not agree in *everything* or go *always* together, or have *no* comparable other friendship of the same intimacy.[54]

6 Santayana as a Literary Critic

PHILOSOPHERS ARE NOT generally noted for their literary criticism, just as literary critics have rarely distinguished themselves as philosophers. For all its integrity, the philosophic mind always runs the danger of becoming too tendentious: it knows too much and cannot become as a little child. On the other hand, the literary mind all too often resembles the ghost of Hamlet's father: 'tis here, 'tis there, a perturbed and insubstantial spirit that flits about in mysterious darkness. It is a rare genius who can combine good philosophy with good literary criticism. Santayana was a genius of this sort.

One is tempted to say that his genius was preeminently of this sort, and that in the special province of philosophical literary criticism his achievement was more clearly unique and permanently outstanding than in any other field. In the past two hundred years there may have been better philosophers and better essayists, and certainly better poets and novelists, but hardly any critics who have blended philosophical and literary insights with as free and authentic a hand as Santayana. Even among the greatest literary critics there have been few who could do the work that Santayana did.

Just what kind of work was it? The practice is almost lost among American writers. In the twentieth century our philosophers and critics alike became technical, minute, and pedagogical in a way that Santayana never was. Ours is an age of instruments: we are devoted to examining the telescope, as Santayana would say, instead of looking through it. Santayana wanted to look. He was an intellectual astronomer with good eyesight and a refined sense of distance. Unlike recent critics, he was not particularly interested in the principles of rhetoric. For better or for worse, his criticism avoids both exegesis and linguistic analysis. He shows how the Homeric Hymns, for instance, exemplify the imaginative function of religion, but he largely ignores the poetic devices they employ. He defines religion in terms of myth and metaphor, but he never provides a thorough analysis of either myth or metaphor. Except for a few remarks about euphony and euphemism, he has little to say about the rudiments of poetry. What excites the muse in him, and what makes his criticism so exciting, is rather an understanding of the human significance of literature—the way in which it can be used to communicate a sense of what is real and important.

Santayana wished to treat literary works of art as expressions of an attitude toward the world that could be examined and criticized, not merely accepted or rejected. In this attempt he tried to make his astronomical reports as comprehensive as possible. He filled them with philosophical commentary reinforced by psychological insights, historical and biographical observations, and the flavor of his own moral and aesthetic taste. All this contributes to a ricochet of ideas, a cross fire that is brilliant, even astounding—so much so that the prose sometimes explodes in a burst of elegance and one has difficulty separating the literary criticism from partisan maneuvering on the one hand and stylistic fireworks on the other.

Comparison with Hegel is inevitable, and in the preface to *The Life of Reason* Santayana reports that the first suggestion for that work came to him after reading the *Phaenomenologie des Geistes*. At the same time, however, Santayana claims that Hegel approached their common subject, the history of ideas, with sophistry and Romantic madness. A similar complaint could not be made against Santayana, whatever his critical or philosophical faults may have been. He never thought that his astronomy disclosed a universe governed by Germanic (or other) orderliness, and he never allowed his own perspective to cripple and cramp everything else in the name of Universal Will. There were marches *in* history, but no march *of* history. If anything, history was a series of aimless dances. One had to catch their individual rhythms, one had to use what Keats called "negative capability" instead of forcing everything into the Hegelian three-step.

All the same, there is one respect in which Santayana resembled Hegel: he had a definite point of view. Like Hegel, Santayana wrote within the framework of a personal philosophy that made up his telescope more than he may always have admitted. In giving his "excuse" for writing about the three philosophical poets, Santayana says that "they have revealed to me certain aspects of nature and of philosophy which I am prompted by mere sincerity to express."[1] But as we read on, we find that these "aspects of nature and of philosophy" turn out to be aspects within Santayana's own nature and philosophy. The philosophical poets have not been chosen at random; they serve a definite philosophical purpose, however little they may be forced to *sub*serve it. Santayana's intention, I am sure, was to choose in accordance with his personal and doctrinal needs, but having chosen, to report accurately and honestly what he saw. His criticism would then be a projection of himself without being a distortion of his subject matter.

Treating Santayana's criticism as an emanation from his own philosophy, we must always remember that the climate of his opinions altered as he grew older. In some ways it became warmer, more tolerant and less demanding; in other ways, colder, more remote and detached from ordinary human interests. For instance, compare "The Poetry of Barbarism" (1900) with "Penitent Art" (1922). In both essays Santayana is describing what he considers to be important but inferior art, the work of strangely misguided talent. But where the earlier essay almost sounds like a cavalry charge against the dark, irrational forces of Whitman's sensualism and Browning's activism, the later essay is a melancholy sigh, a gentle shaking of the deploring head, as if Santayana had come to see that it is only fitting for the tragic twentieth century to present itself in an abstract, incomplete, and self-caricaturing manner.

Similarly, in "The Absence of Religion in Shakespeare" (1906) Santayana is shocked to find that Shakespeare has little of what might be considered cosmic awareness, whereas in "Tragic Philosophy" (1936) he is more tolerant of a poet who spoke to an age that "needed . . . no mastering living religion."[2] It is not clear whether the later Santayana finds Shakespeare's secularism inadequate for the demands of great poetry; but as against the criticism of T. S. Eliot, he defends Shakespeare for having "stuck fast in the facts of life," and he pits him against Dante in a way that one could hardly have anticipated from the early essay.[3]

Throughout this changing climate, there perseveres a way of looking at things, a prevailing sensibility or general perspective, that articulates a desire to harmonize. In book after book, Santayana defined the life of reason as the harmonization between opposing interests. In his aesthetics and literary criticism he works out patterns of harmonization among a great many divergent principles, most of which can be approached in relation to the following themes: Platonism vs. naturalism, classicism vs. romanticism, "idealisation" vs. realism, and poetry vs. prose. Although each conflict poses separate problems, the problems overlap, and much of what we say about one will also apply to the others.

The struggle in Santayana's literary criticism between naturalism and Platonism is the most striking of the four themes. Throughout all his work there is that ambivalence of sentiment I have discussed, a yearning toward the extremes of naturalism with its emphasis upon the brute materiality of existent things and Platonism with its reliance upon the value of formal characteristics. Trying to harness both, the black horse of the body and the white horse of the soul, Santayana wanted them to run in neatly parallel lines. In order to effect this harmonization, he used each pole to chasten the other. They were the two masks of his drama, and his prose bristles with their dialogue.

Speaking in the person of naturalism, he attacks Platonism for being superstitious and absurdly optimistic. Because there are human values in the world, Platonism assumes that ideal entities, or purposive divinities as Christianity made them into, must yield the ultimate explanation for the existence of everything. Nothing could be further from the materialistic truth. But speaking in the person of reconstituted Platonism, Santayana reviles traditional naturalism as barren of hope and ignorant of spiritual goods. Devoted as it is to facts, naturalism tends to neglect the fact of human aspiration and the quest for purified ideals.

In *The Last Puritan*, where the spirituality of Oliver Alden is pitted against the naturalism of Mario Van de Weyer, the contrast between the two sides of Santayana's nature shows itself in a scene I have not yet mentioned. Oliver is completing an essay on Plato's *Symposium*. As his hand writes the word *philosophy*, he is interrupted by Mario, who describes an unhappy sexual encounter he has just had and then boards a train on his way to help his dying mother. Oliver returns to his room and finds that he has failed to put down the last five letters of *philosophy*. Thus, as philosophy is split into its two halves, of love and wisdom, and Mario pursues the one while Oliver is arrested as usual in his search for the other, so too is man composed of matter and spirit as two separate, warring elements in his being. Santayana's thinking always has its feet on the ground and its head in the clouds. Whether there is, or ought to be, anything in between remains a matter of controversy.

The character of Santayana's naturalism is reflected in his essays on Lucretius and Dickens. Explaining the sense in which Lucretius is a "poet of matter," Santayana distinguishes among five different kinds of "naturalists" in poetry. Lucretius is a philosophical or cosmological naturalist—for him nature means "the principle of birth or genesis, the universal mother, the great cause, or system of causes."[4] As a philosophical naturalist, Lucretius is contrasted with the descriptive poet, who paints a word picture of the scenery of nature; the symbolist poet, who breaks up nature into units that he reshuffles by means of random association; the idealist poet, who uses these bits of nature to construct a utopian dreamworld; and the humanist poet, who portrays the moral effects that can be derived from living "in" nature.

These are all naturalists, but second-rate. The descriptive poet ignores Lessing's scruples about representing spatial objects in a temporal medium; the symbolists "play with things luxuriously, making them symbols for their thoughts, instead of mending their thoughts intelligently, to render them symbols for things"; the idealist poet is blind to the dynamism of matter; the humanist poet, such as Wordsworth, limits himself to a tiny part of the cosmic process. Only a poet like Lucretius has his finger on the pulse of nature, its character as a force, a power, a generating and destroying agency. Only Lucretius, we may add, concerns himself with what Santayana later called the "Realm of Matter." As Santayana praises Lucretius for writing "the poetry of things themselves" he calls himself, in "Apologia Pro Mente Sua" (1940), a "true poet" inasmuch as his own poetry is "not a poetry of words or concepts, but a poetry of things."[5]

Is this sufficient for elevating Lucretius above Wordsworth and the symbolists? That a kinship of perception should make Lucretius dearer to Santayana is not at all surprising, but Santayana does not appear to be expressing an idiosyncratic preference. He seems to be evaluating poetry in terms of objective standards of criticism. This problem recurs continually in his writing.

Since philosophical naturalism investigates the principles of genesis and decay, the essay on Lucretius hovers about the dualism of life and death, creation and destruction, peace and war, love and strife, as symbolized in De Rerum Natura by Venus and Mars. This awareness of the "double colouring" of things appears in all of Santayana's work. In "A Long Way Round to Nirvana" he defends the Freudian notion that a universal death drive counterbalances the striving for self-preservation. Like all philosophy, belief in a death drive had to be taken as a metaphoric suggestion, not as scientific truth, but correctly interpreted that idea refers to something that Santayana applauds as a fair report of "the general movement and the pertinent issue of material facts."[6]

In emphasizing death as one of the facts of life, Santayana's philosophy wears the same tragic cast as European existentialism. He wished to construct his system on the basis of a radical disillusionment. Once human beings *realized* that they are dust, that there is no other world, and that someday they will be dead 100 percent, they could freely and staunchly search for the good. Santayana felt that it would be cheating for us to be bribed into virtue by hopes of a future life or by optimistic assurances that the good wins out eventually. There was no prearranged harmony, no ultimate dialectic, no *élan vital* that guaranteed anything. Death and evil were as indigenous to nature as life and goodness. They were to be observed and studied, not wished out of existence.

In *Three Philosophical Poets* this naturalistic analysis takes up much of the essay on Lucretius and functions in the succeeding ones on Dante and Goethe. The Paolo-Francesca scene, for instance, is presented as a continuation of Lucretius on Mars and Venus. Paolo and Francesca are in hell because their union is unnatural, as intimacy must always be when it makes separateness and individuality impossible. An eternity of possession in a void, of inescapable love and no exit into anything or anyone else, causes the destruction of Mars in a manner that prevents Venus from savoring her conquest. "Only an inspired poet could be so subtle a moralist," Santayana states. "Only a sound moralist could be so tragic a poet."[7]

Similarly, Mephistopheles in *Faust* is compared to the Mars of Lucretius, and Santayana delights in Goethe's ability to depict the nothingness of things by means of him. Santayana denies that Mephistopheles can be fitted into a Hegelian dialectic, as the naysaying that makes a higher yea-saying possible and thus unintentionally furthers the good. On the one hand, Santayana sees the sense in which Mephistopheles is consciously, not unintentionally, benevolent. For Mephistopheles destruction is better than creation, and it is destruction that he knowingly and gladly chooses. On the other hand, Santayana refuses to bleach the blackness of Mephistopheles. Creation is one thing; destruction is another. Sentimentality or barbaric romanticism results from confusing the two, from making the colors run so that neither has a determinate quality of its own.

It is a comparable desire to affirm the irreducibility of black and white, or any other hues, that Santayana admires most in Dickens. He finds in him the same love of common people that Walt Whitman had, except that Dickens is free of all impressionistic wishy-washiness. Whitman interpreted everything else in terms of himself, but Dickens perceived the differences in things. Unlike Whitman, Dickens saw life as "a concourse of very distinct, individual bodies, natural and social, each with its definite interests and story."[8] This naturalistic clear-headedness enabled him to sympathize with the aspirations of others, to love "the love in everything" as Santayana says in "Ultimate Religion," without forgetting that vice is really vice and must be annihilated for the greater good of humankind.[9]

In taking Dickens as an outstanding example of uncontaminated naturalism, Santayana also sees him as the prototype of comedy in general. Comedy sees things externally, as mere occurrences in nature that have no necessary reason for being. The existence of everything is, as the existentialists say, "absurd"—we can never prove deductively that anything must or must not be. Comedy cuts beneath convention in order to show the absurdity of existence, thereby revealing its fundamental materiality. Comedy requires courage, and is usually cruel. Dickens had the courage, but not the cruelty. Santayana praises him for combining naturalistic insight with a universal kindliness that tempers his savage strokes and allows readers to enjoy the comic spectacle in which they are themselves participants.

If Santayana's naturalistic mask is comic, his Platonic one is tragic.

As a naturalist, Santayana joins with Sancho Panza in laughing at misadventures that result from neglecting the facts of daily life; as a Platonist, he feels the compelling pathos of a Don Quixote whose madness flows directly from his sense of what is good. In the preface to *The Last Puritan* Santayana complains that the critics have misunderstood the tragedy of his hero. That Oliver died young or was killed in an accident did not make him tragic, but rather his having stopped himself, "not trusting his inspiration."[10] And in "Tragic Philosophy" Santayana writes that tragedy is the "conflict between inspiration and truth."[11] Tragedy shows us men and women from their own inward point of view, as they are motivated by desires and aspirations that are serious to them, not at all absurd, though more or less doomed to failure. Human life is tragic because it always seeks to attain ideals that, in the nature of our reality, can never be fully attained. For the Platonist the actual world is inevitably the scene of tragedy.

Santayana's Platonism is most thoroughly expressed in his essays on "Platonic Love in Some Italian Poets," "Dante," and "Shelley." Each deals with Platonism in a different setting; and each displays the critic in a somewhat different posture. In the first essay, Santayana recites the story of Beatrice and Dante, and then shrewdly reminds us that despite his lifelong devotion Dante took a wife just as Beatrice had taken a husband. Did Dante's marriage satisfy his naturalistic needs and thus release him for the more important love of an ideal? Or did it force him into a "species of infidelity" toward Beatrice as well as his wife? Santayana never gives us a straight answer. He documents the achievement of the Platonizing Italian poets, and he praises their intense contemplation, which "disentangles the ideal from the idol of sense." At the same time, he also understands that Platonic love is based upon pervasive frustration. The beauties that attract the Platonist by suggesting the ideal must always fail to satisfy because they do not fulfill it.[12] Platonism fascinates Santayana by the purity of its transcendence, but he is too this-worldly to drop his naturalism completely.

In his chapter on "Dante" as the second of the philosophical poets, Santayana seems sharper in his criticism and more enthusiastic in his praise. Like Christianity itself, Dante offends him by having turned Platonism into a historical drama, making it the kind of *super-naturalism* that Santayana could not abide. Dante evinces all the imperfections of what he deems Christian superstition, such as the belief in original sin and retributive justice. Finally, Santayana asserts that Dante was dedicated to a kind of love that is neither normal nor healthy nor natural nor manly; and he adds that "the poet who wishes to pass convincingly from love to philosophy (and that seems a natural progress for a poet) should accordingly be a hearty and complete lover—a lover like Goethe and his Faust—rather than like Plato and Dante." But these naturalistic complaints are only one side of the coin. The reverse is pure eulogy. The merits of Dante's worldview are said to redeem all his defects, for they are the merits of the Platonizing imagination writ large, of the sense of good and evil operating on a cosmic scale. The chapter ends with Santayana putting Dante forth as "a successful example of the *highest species* of poetry."[13]

The essay on Shelley is more serene than the other two. One feels that Santayana's philosophical position had developed to a point where he was more confident of reconciling the best of Platonism with the best of naturalism. And it is evident that in Shelley he finds the best of Platonism. He speaks of Shelley as a pure, winged spirit whose love of the ideal was sincere and spontaneous. Shelley was not limited by Christian beliefs, and his Platonism resulted from sympathy with the misery of everything in nature rather than from personal disappointment. Although he was ignorant of the dynamic workings of matter, Shelley knew what was good and bad in things. If his poetry demolished the everyday world, it was only to rebuild it in a playful, selfless way "nearer to the heart's desire."[14]

Shelley's idealism is the same as the idealistic naturalism that Santayana had earlier compared to Lucretius's philosophical naturalism.
As a kind of naturalism, he there considered it inferior to what
Lucretius gives us. But as a type of idealism, he now admires it as
supreme poetry. Dickens and Shelley, between them, seem to make
up Santayana's vision, just as Lucretius and Dante do. Dickens rol-
licks through the natural world, above which the skylark Shelley
soars in search of universal freedom; Lucretius hears the voice of
things themselves while Dante documents the uses to which spirit
can put them.

In moving to our second theme, we are confronted by questions of
interpretation that did not arise in the first. Although it is obvious
that Santayana wishes to stereoscope the partial views of naturalism and Platonism, it is not immediately evident that he wants to
do the same with classicism and romanticism. Santayana is known
as the defender of the one and the critic of the other, and much
could be cited in favor of this reading. Nevertheless, it is a superficial interpretation that has to be greatly subtilized before it can be
accepted. For one thing, we ought not to confuse "barbarism," as
Santayana calls it, with romanticism in its entirety. Barbarism is only
one kind of romanticism. It is romanticism that refuses to be harmonized. The barbarian is "the man who does not know his deriv-
ations nor perceive his tendencies, but who merely feels and acts,
valuing in his life its force and its filling, but being careless of its purpose and its form."[15] The romanticist values the experiential flow
of his life; he becomes a barbarian when he values nothing else,
when he *merely* feels and acts. Hence it is barbarism, and not necessarily romanticism, that is incompatible with the classical sense of
purpose and form that Santayana wants to advocate.

Santayana's attack upon nineteenth-century barbarism is guided by the same kind of historical or sociological outlook that T. S. Eliot took as a premise of his own literary criticism. Examining barbaric poetry "in relation to the general moral crisis and imaginative disintegration of which it gives a verbal echo," Santayana notes that the imagination of Western man bears a duality of inspiration.[16] It derives in part from classical literature, in part from Christianity. The confusion of barbaric poetry manifests the modern inability to serve both masters, or either one, or any other.

Santayana calls Whitman and Browning "poets of barbarism" because they reject each tradition without really understanding it and without having anything to put in its place. They revel in sensations and emotions without fitting them into a rational system of any sort. To Santayana's ear and eye they are like the players Hamlet describes as created by nature's journeymen: "neither having the accent of Christians nor the gait of Christian, pagan, nor man."[17] Even when it studies the past, as historicism does, barbarism examines a corpse instead of communicating with a vital tradition. If history preoccupies modern poets, Santayana reminds his readers at the turn of the century, it is because they are so vastly conscious of a separation from the past.

That Santayana's comments about barbarism are not intended to cover all Romantic poetry is revealed by his treatment of Goethe, whom he ranks with Dante and Lucretius rather than with Whitman and Browning. The saving grace of Goethe, as Santayana sees him, is his real and genuine effort to fit romanticism into a framework of classicism. *Faust* is a return to Lucretius, though with a difference. What differs is the emphasis on life itself, on "experience in its immediacy, variety, and apparent groundlessness."[18]

This is what all romanticism emphasizes, but Santayana believes that in Goethe it is accompanied by moments of sad and classic wisdom. One of these occurs when Faust calls forth the Earth-Spirit, the symbol of unlimited and indiscriminate experience. The ugly spectacle of unformed and disorganized life in all its infinite variations horrifies Faust. He learns, as Eliot would say, that "human kind / Cannot bear very much reality," that the life of *mere* experience is not worth living.[19] To be happy one must recognize the limits of one's nature, one must temper the fervor of youth with the discipline of age, one must make oneself by means of freely calculated choice. This is the classical point of view, and it is the morality Santayana expounded throughout his life.

If this classical side of Goethe redeems him in the eyes of Santayana, it is nevertheless too meager to raise him as high as Lucretius and Dante. In drawing his conclusions, Santayana orders the three philosophical poets hierarchically. At the top stands Dante, the poet of salvation; next, Lucretius, the poet of nature; and at the bottom, Goethe, the poet of life. The basis of this arrangement is not entirely clear. On the one hand, Santayana specifically denies that he is trying to determine which of the poets is best: "Each is the best in his way, and none is the best in every way. To express a preference is not so much a criticism as a personal confession." Just three pages later, however, he sounds as if his hierarchy is based on something more objective than his own taste: "Taken formally, and in respect to their type of philosophy and imagination, Dante is on a higher plane than Lucretius, and Lucretius on a higher plane than Goethe."[20]

Without pausing to examine the difficulties in Santayana's statement, we should here notice that his hierarchy places the representative of Platonism first and the representative of romanticism last. Though Santayana wants to harmonize Platonism with naturalism and classicism with romanticism, he insists upon a specific kind of harmonization, one in which naturalism is subordinate to Platonism and romanticism to classicism.

This implicit standard leads Santayana, in the early essays at least, to place Shakespeare below the level of Homer, Virgil, and Dante. Like Goethe, Shakespeare is a Romantic poet but not a poet of barbarism. Although he is "not unacquainted with speculation," Shakespeare generally restricts himself to the poetry of ordinary experience: he chooses positivism rather than religion, and society rather than the cosmos. Even in the case of *Hamlet,* "here is no necessary human tragedy, no universal destiny or divine law." Santayana does concede that Hamlet reveals "much of what is deepest and rarest in human feeling."[21] But if this is so, why not admit the supremely philosophical excellence of Shakespeare? Granted that he is not philosophical in the same sense in which Lucretius and Dante are, why not acknowledge his equally profound understanding of everything there is to understand?

The answer to these questions turns on Santayana's imperfect appreciation of romanticism. In subordinating it to classicism, he misconstrues, and possibly ignores, the problems that most profoundly troubled the Romantics. Lamenting the absence of religion in Shakespeare, Santayana overlooks the fact that Shakespeare's philosophic insight had a different configuration. Shakespeare, like Goethe, like Whitman and Browning, and like a great many other modern writers, saw the world in terms of moral and interpersonal problems. Religion did not concern him greatly since it was unable to settle the ethical dilemmas that structured this perspective. Hamlet, similar to all of Shakespeare's major characters in that regard, is tormented by problems of action that the playwright analyzes with a remarkable degree of precision.

Likewise, one could interpret the trial of Faust in terms of the need to *do* something. Mephistopheles is to win his wager if he can debase Faust's vital energy to a level at which he will do virtually anything; Faust drops dead when he acquiesces in the passing moment; his soul is saved because, until the advent of his death, he is unflagging in his active aspiration. The paradigm of all romanticism was formulated by Schopenhauer when he defined the human lot as the sorrowful alternation between need and boredom. The bored man has nothing for which to act; the needful man is forced to act in any way that will relieve his discomfiture. How then can human beings truly act with freedom? How can they have intelligence and spontaneous goodwill? How can they ever experience a life of meaning and positive happiness? These questions did not affect Santayana as a philosopher in the way that problems of belief did. It is fortunate that he pursued his own vision. But it prevented him from penetrating to the deepest stratum of the Romantic soul.[22]

❋

The next theme takes us into the critical theory that underlies most of Santayana's practice. His preference for classicism over romanticism, as well as his preference for Platonism over naturalism, issues from his conception of idealization. As a principle of aesthetic valuation, it runs through all his criticism but receives full treatment only in *The Sense of Beauty*.

To explain what Santayana means by idealization in this context, we must first see its derivation from his general aesthetics. At the very outset Santayana defines the aesthetic in terms of "objectified pleasure"—that is, pleasure that is experienced as an attribute of an object more or less in the way that its color is. According to Santayana, the difference between "this painting pleases me" and "this painting is beautiful" consists in the fact that the first statement describes an effect that the painting has upon the speaker, whereas the second statement treats the painting as itself embodying the pleasure it causes. To the literal, scientific mind it makes no sense to speak of an object embodying pleasures; but the aesthetic is neither literal nor scientific. Santayana takes it to be a hangover from the primitive, animistic tendency to read into objects all of the effects they have upon human experience. The sense of beauty causes us to project our feelings and perceptions without realizing what we are doing. To this extent, Santayana would say, all art is illusion.

There is, however, a further dimension of art that is more relevant to idealization as Santayana portrays it. After suggesting that beauty is objectified pleasure, Santayana goes on to discuss three different kinds of beauty: the beauty of materials, of form, and of expression. Of these three the greatest is form, and in the aesthetics of form the most significant factor is the creation of types—the class concepts or general ideas through which we identify particular objects. Types are especially important to artists because they enable them to remain true to observation without copying, without duplicating something that has existed and therefore possesses an indefinite number of properties that are aesthetically irrelevant.

Analyzing the nature of types, Santayana rejects the Platonic view that considers them independent of ordinary sense experience. Santayana insists that a type—the general idea of man, tree, whale, or whatnot—is merely a lowest common denominator, a residue of sense data that appear on particular occasions. When Santayana later developed the doctrine of essences, he moved closer to Platonism inasmuch as he denied that the naturalistic origin of types kept them from being ontologically prior to experience. What remained constant in both the earlier and the later theories was the belief that typical form is the most important kind of aesthetic form.

Now we are in position to understand how Santayana conceives of idealization in art, and how he reconciles it with aesthetic truth. Having defined beauty in terms of pleasure, and typical form in terms of observable recurrences, Santayana then says that typical form can have its greatest effect only if it is modified "in the direction of the observer's pleasure" and thereby turned into an "idealisation." This means that artists must not content themselves with a purely realistic portrayal of types, any more than with a realistic representation of some actual object. The former would be an un-aesthetic copy as much as the latter, albeit a copy of "the average of things" rather than of specific attributes of particular entities. The sense of beauty being the experience of pleasure in the object, the sense of formal beauty must be the experience of a type that has been modified for the sake of giving greater pleasure. "The mind is thus peopled by general ideas in which beauty is the chief quality; and these ideas are at the same time the types of things."[23]

In this manner, Santayana hopes to combine our sense of reality with our sense of beauty. A mere sense of reality would disclose typical forms that might very well be harsh, shocking, brutal. A mere sense of beauty would provide abstract or wholly fanciful enjoyment. But when the forms themselves have been modified in the direction of pleasure, they incorporate pertinent ideals while also depicting human realities. Santayana insists that these ideals are "true to" reality since they have been fashioned as refinements of forms that truly matter rather than as phantasmagoria invented by a raving artist. They are much more significant than the photographs of nature that so-called realists provide.

Thus, despite his emphasis on idealization, Santayana does not wish to ignore the artistic importance of truth. When he discusses the nature of expression in literature, he reminds us that great works often employ accurate and penetrating representation. But having said this, he quickly adds that "such instruction does not of itself constitute an aesthetic pleasure: the other conditions of beauty remain to be fulfilled."[24] These other conditions are realized only when the vehicle, the art object, provides pleasure in its direct effect, which is to say that the presentation of truth cannot be aesthetic unless it furthers the beauty of form and materials. And since the beauty of form is at its highest when it employs idealization, the superlative work of art will have to subordinate its realistic elements to the creation of ideal types.

In a comparable vein Santayana denies that the expression of evil can be aesthetic in itself. He goes to great lengths to show that tragedies are aesthetic only in spite of the evil they represent, never because of it. The expression of evil is unpleasant, therefore unaesthetic, and so the tragedian must always cushion it by means of pleasing idealizations. With this theory in mind, it is predictable that Santayana would prefer Platonism and classicism to naturalism and romanticism.

When he applies his theories about ideal types to the special problem of characterization, Santayana enriches them by saying that the great characters of literature are always individuals as well as idealizations. Universal figures like Hamlet, Don Quixote, Achilles are not just particular persons candidly observed. Nor are they averages or realistic types. They are idealized types that have been given uniqueness or individuality. Goethe's Gretchen had no original, but is herself the original. It is here that Santayana repeats Aristotle's dictum that "poetry is truer than history."[25]

Santayana's conception of idealization also underlies his celebrated identification of religion with poetry. As he sees it, religion is primarily poetic idealization extended to the cosmos as a whole. "Poetry is called religion when it intervenes in life, and religion, when it merely supervenes upon life, is seen to be nothing but poetry."[26] Santayana knows that religious people have not usually *thought* that their religion is a kind of elevated poetry. They have usually taken it to be a superior science. This side of religion he repudiates as sheer superstition.

In classifying religion with poetry, Santayana is trying to release imaginative values that can remain to the enlightened and sensitive intellect after all pseudoscientific claims have been discounted. He relates this residue to idealization because he thinks that a religion fulfills its function only by symbolizing desired perfections. The religion of Apollo he extols as a true religion because it expressed a sense of moral values and vividly portrayed the ideal in relation to its "natural ground." He suggests that the Christ people love is "an ideal of their own hearts"; and he asserts that "no poet has ever equalled the perfection or significance of these religious creations."[27]

The trouble with Santayana's theory of idealization is that it seems to minimize the importance of objective truth. Idealizations do not tell us how things are but how they ought to be, or how the "heart's desire" would like them to be. If aesthetic excellence depends on idealization, art is oriented toward wish fulfillment more than anything else. As long as we concern ourselves with the artist's idealization, we are not especially interested in anything he tells us about the world; what matters most is his dream of perfection, his prophetic blueprint. If realism ignores ideals, it will have to be curtailed. If tragedy expresses sad and bitter truths, it will have to do so in a way that is ultimately pleasurable and uplifting. Dante idealizes to the fullest. He is therefore called "the type of a supreme poet." Lucretius, Goethe, and Shakespeare idealize proportionately less, and they are fitted into the hierarchy of value accordingly. Santayana never faces up to the possibility that a priori there is no reason to favor idealization over realism, and he fails to see how his preferred kind of harmonization distorts much of what is ordinarily thought to be essential in both poetry and religion.

Related difficulties attend Santayana's mode of reconciling poetry with prose. Santayana begins with the assumption that poetry and prose are two different types of discourse: the former devoted to the sound and texture of words, and to the experience they can evoke or symbolize; the latter designed for practical use in the material environment. Poetry gives us the world in its immediacy; prose tells us about it discursively. Poetry portrays life as it flows;

prose does the very opposite—as in science or in philosophy, it theorizes and tries to understand.

How then are the two to be joined? Santayana is convinced that neither poetry nor prose can accomplish its aesthetic mission without the other. He criticizes the shallow aestheticism that decrees that art and reason are incompatible, and that poetry must ignore the problems of the real world. The "rational poet" whom Santayana deifies throughout his early writing unites intelligence with imagination: "A rational poet's vision would have the same moral functions which myth was asked to fulfill, and fulfilled so treacherously. . . . His poetry, without ceasing to be a fiction in its method and ideality, would be an ultimate truth in its practical scope."[28] Such poetry succeeds by digesting prose, by putting it to aesthetic employment rather than spewing it forth.

But just how is the harmonization between poetry and prose effected? Santayana returns to the problem in the introduction to *Three Philosophical Poets.* He wonders whether poetry is capable of supporting the analytical reasoning of philosophy. He replies that it cannot, and that it should not try to do so, and yet that philosophical poetry is poetry at its best. He concludes that philosophy itself is poetic to the extent that it terminates in "a steady contemplation of all things in their order and worth."[29]

Santayana dedicated much of his later philosophy to the study of contemplation in this sense. It consists in the intuition of essences. In his note on Proust, he says that an essence is "the recognizable character of any object or feeling, all of it that can actually be possessed in sensation or recovered in memory, or transcribed in art, or conveyed to another mind."[30] To discover essences one had to limit oneself to experience as it comes, experience devoid of interpretation and the interpretative processes of reason. In conveying a complex essence of things in their order and worth, philosophical poetry would remain nondiscursive, and therefore distinctively poetical, at the same time as it included the overarching visions of philosophy. Poetry is the language of intuition, according to Santayana. In being harmonized with prose, it becomes the language of significant, and possibly truthful, insights.

Though fully developed only late in Santayana's life, the doctrine of essences lurks within most of his literary criticism. I have tried elsewhere to show that it is basic to all his theories of art and aesthetics.[31] I also believe that it renders most of them philosophically suspect. Here I need only suggest that Santayana's reliance upon intuition subordinates the ordinary processes of thought to a kind of quasi-mystical state whose philosophical validity one may question from various points of view. And even if it makes sense to speak of contemplation in the way that Santayana does, one may still wonder how any of this is relevant to either art or the definition of great poetry. That philosophical poetry depends on general ideas about the world is readily admissible; but that these ideas are intuitions of a unique and inherently nondiscursive sort may only be an arbitrary article of faith.

The nature of Santayana's faith is indicated by the extent to which the doctrine of essences led him to alter his earlier aesthetics. At some points, the revisions were minor; at others, extensive. In modifying his definition of beauty, he said that he still adhered to its major import and was mainly changing the language. He no longer felt the necessity of talking about the objectification of pleasure because on the doctrine of essences pleasure "does not need to be objectified in order to be fused into an image felt to be beautiful: if felt at all, pleasure is already an object of intuition."[32] The ideal of an aesthetic attitude that would be at once intuitive and pleasurable had always been present in Santayana's thinking. The theory of essences gave him a new, and more original, way of formulating his conception.

On questions about aesthetic excellence and the importance of philosophical poetry, however, Santayana's later thinking differed sharply from his former view. His change of heart sounds almost like a recantation:

> So anxious was I, when younger, to find some rational justification for poetry and religion, and to show that their magic was significant of true facts, that I insisted too much, as I now think, on the need of relevance to fact even in poetry. Not only did I distinguish good religion from bad by its expression of practical wisdom and of the moral discipline that makes for happiness in this world, but I maintained that the noblest poetry also must express the moral burden of life and must be rich in wisdom. Age has made me less exacting, and I can now find quite sufficient perfection in poetry, like that of the Chinese and Arabians, without much philosophic scope, in mere grace and feeling and music and cloud-castles and frolic. . . . When living substance is restored beneath the surface of experience, there is no longer any reason for assuming that the first song of a bird may not be infinitely rich and as deep as heaven, if it utters the vital impulses of that moment with enough completeness. The analogies of this utterance with other events, or its outlying suggestions, whilst they may render it more intelligible to a third person, would not add much to its inward force and intrinsic beauty. Its lyric adequacy, though of course not independent of nature, would be independent of wisdom. If besides being an adequate expression of the soul, the song expressed the lessons of a broad experience, which that soul had gathered and digested, this fact certainly would lend a great tragic sublimity to that song; but to be poetical or religious intrinsically, the mystic cry is enough.[33]

This statement appeared in 1922, eleven years after *Three Philosophical Poets*. Almost all of Santayana's literary criticism having been written before the twenties, the later standard had virtually no effect upon it. Though essays such as "Penitent Art," "Tragic Philosophy," and "Literary Psychology" reflect the final doctrine, Santayana never attempted to reconstruct his youthful criticism. It is therefore extremely difficult to say just how much of his great writings on literature the older Santayana would readily have retained. And what would his essays have been like if he had used the later rather than the earlier standard? The question is beguiling, as such questions always are. But perhaps we do best to leave it as a question. Speculation in this matter would be thoroughly inconclusive.

7   Greatness in Art

IN THE ROLE OF literary critic as well as philosopher, Santayana is much concerned about the nature of artistic excellence.
The standards he employs are never explicitly stated but may easily be reconstructed from his opinions about the aesthetic effects
of different works of art. The four levels of poetry that Santayana
describes in *Interpretations of Poetry and Religion* are especially ger-
mane. His literary criticism was, to a considerable degree, written
with this classification in mind. He analyzes the subject matter and

techniques of the poets with whom he deals, classifies their work in terms of the four levels, and evaluates accordingly. But as he develops the doctrine of essence, his critical theory changes, and his criterion of excellence becomes significantly different from what it was before.

The first level of poetry, which Santayana describes in the early essay "The Elements and Function of Poetry," is the level at which sheer sound is most important. The lowest common denominator, the stuff of poetry, is words; and sound is the chief sensuous material of words. On this level euphony is the principal value. Since poetry is virtual music, the highest form of euphony is song. But human speech has sacrificed song to the exigencies of communication. All that remains, therefore, is the euphony in vowels and consonants and in the rhythm of discourse—euphony that results from the succession of sounds and the effects of rhyme and meter.

Talent or ability on this level has the same relation to great poetry, Santayana declares, as "scales and aimless warblings bear to great singing—they test the essential endowment and fineness of the organ which is to be employed in the art." Euphonious effects are nevertheless essential to great poetry, for they provide the sensory foundation and basic musical quality. To illustrate this element of poetry, Santayana cites passages from Shelley's "Revolt of Islam" and Keats's "Endymion" that do not convey any definite meaning but only "a kind of objectless passion which is little more than the sensation of the movement and sensuous richness of the lines."[1] On the following page, however, he admits that in these words there is already more than just sound and meter. That brings him to the second level.

The characteristic of poetry on this level Santayana calls euphuism, by which he means "the choice of coloured words and rare and elliptical phrases . . . the fanciful, rich, or exquisite juxtaposition of phrases."[2] Their combination of precious vocabulary and highly exquisite style explains why the lines from Keats and Shelley were actually poetic, albeit on a low level. The lack of euphuism in the following couplet by Pope leads Santayana to conclude that mere euphony does not make poetry:

> In spite of pride, in erring reason's spite,
> One truth is clear, Whatever is, is right.

Here there is no grievous fault of sound or meter, and yet, according to Santayana, "we should hesitate to say that such writing was truly poetical."[3] Although the required element of euphony is present, the couplet is "too intellectual": exact reference interests Pope more than any rich and fanciful suggestion. Pope makes insufficient use of vague words and elusive meanings, and of the emotive quality that poetic language should possess. The nineteenth-century Symbolists, on the other hand, lean so heavily on the device of euphuism, Santayana claims, that they tend to overlook the other levels that poetry can include.

In reaching the third level, we definitely move beyond the rudiments of verse. Poetry on this level is more complex than merely euphonious or euphuistic discourse, but it too concentrates upon a distinctive aspect of poetry in general—the imaginative and intuitive appreciation of essences. The art form depicts what is given in immediate experience. Instead of accepting commonsense beliefs, the poet reduces them to the intuitions from which they originated. He conveys the impact of sensuous phenomena, not the conceptualization of substance. Having surrendered all desire either to understand the world or to act within it, the poet collects and records sensory impressions that our intellect can neither portray nor utilize without distortion. Indulging in the pathetic fallacy, he or she restores to whatever object is being considered the emotional quality with which a child or primitive adult experiences it. Since poetry on this level is a mode of communication, it must involve some type of representation. But what the poet represents (or intends, as Santayana would probably say) is not substance or the content of any belief, but rather a complexity of essences. The poet is not interested in providing what Santayana calls "information."

There are two kinds of essences that Santayana seems to associate with the third level of poetry. The first displays moods and specific images. The poetry of Walt Whitman, Santayana suggests, largely consists in portraying simple qualities as they impinge upon the senses. In Whitman's work we find "the swarms of men and objects rendered as they might strike the retina in a sort of waking dream. It is the most sincere possible confession of the lowest—I mean the most primitive—type of perception."[4] Elsewhere, in the midst of an article on American philosophy, Santayana remarks that Whitman "reduced his imagination to a passive sensorium for the registering of impressions."[5]

The Symbolists, too, we are told, were "fascinated by pure sense," the simple qualities felt in direct experience. In accordance with their emphasis upon euphuism, they did not seek to impart meanings so much as to present a field of qualities associated with some emotion or sensation. "For they play with things luxuriously, making them symbols for their thoughts, instead of mending their thoughts intelligently, to render them symbols for things."[6]

The second type of essence displays passions and the feelings that arise in the course of action. Robert Browning is taken to exemplify the kind of poet who expresses man's passional and erratic nature. More sophisticated than Whitman, Browning is not limited to sensation and the simplest qualities. He depicts intricate sentiments and the excitement of an active life. By means of these essences, he imparts a sense of human character and emotion. Because Browning cannot "rationalize emotion" or recognize how it may be wedded to a more philosophical outlook, Santayana calls his poetry, like Whitman's, barbaric. The barbarian is one who "regards his passions as their own excuse for being; who does not domesticate them either by understanding their cause or by conceiving their ideal goal."[7]

Whitman and Browning are deemed poets of barbarism because they revel in the vividness of rudimentary sensation and strong but undisciplined feeling. With a slight difference, they resemble the artists whom Santayana discusses in "Penitent Art." There he suggests that the fear of reason has caused modern painters either to renounce representation entirely or to offer "a pregnant hint, some large graphic sign, some profound caricature" instead of a complete and explicit portrait of the object.[8]

Correspondingly, Santayana argues that the third level of poetry is no more adequate in itself than either of the previous ones. Its ultimate failure, as evidenced by poetry such as Browning's, results from difficulties inherent in its treatment of the passions. Human character and emotion are of special importance to a poet, but they must be presented in relation to an objective environment and by means of dramatic situations. For imagination to have its fullest and most rewarding function, the outer world must be "bathed in the hues of human feeling, the inner world expressed in the forms of things."[9] In order for poets to satisfy these conditions, they must externalize the emotions, and thus discover the "correlative objects" that will show them forth. This, Santayana concludes, inevitably commits poetry to a wider interpretation of experience than is attempted on the third level.

Santayana's emphasis upon correlative objects brings him to the level of "rational poetry." On this level poetry tries to construct a reasoned and reasonable world outlook. Open to the immediate aspect of experience but not limited to it, the poet knows how to integrate sense and passion into a conception of nature. He employs euphonious and euphuistic devices and seeks to penetrate to the essential and intuitive core that underlies conventional responses. But now the artistic effort is directed toward fashioning a philosophical or religious point of view. At the same time, *as poetry,* the work does not communicate explicit information, and a reader has no need of discursive reason in order to appreciate it.

There are several tasks that rational poets must undertake and complete, according to Santayana. They must subordinate characterization to plot, and therefore portray a personage by depicting the human circumstances in which he or she appears. In order to show the nature and significance of a character, the rational poet resorts to dramatic events and intersubjective occurrences, rather than soliloquizing or introspecting. Like Aristotle, Santayana believes that narrative is the most important element in fiction.

But he also thinks that the rational poet must place the characters within a material and historical setting. The causes and conditions of their emotions can be explained only in terms of their cultural traditions and natural surroundings. Santayana ascribes the greatness of Virgil and Dante to their awareness of the forces at work within their social milieux. All the classic poets, he insists, have "the topographical sense." Instead of representing nature as a landscape painter might, they constantly alert the audience to the natural forces that move heaven and earth and that control society. They describe the countryside not directly, but only through myth and fable. In this way they invoke the cultural and historical import of the place, and that is more significant than listing its physical properties.

Nevertheless, Santayana warns us, a poet may fall into the dangerous practice of delineating the landscape in human terms. He might not catalog the affecting minutiae of an outdoor scene, but he might limit himself to the inspirational or recuperative power that the landscape has upon men and women. Wordsworth is said to fail in this respect. Instead of dealing with "genesis, evolution, and natural force in its myriad manifestations," Wordsworth "dwells on adventitious human matters."[10] A truly philosophical poet makes neither a realistic nor a moral snapshot of nature; he or she locates the scene by means of allusions, generally mythological, that relate it to a way of seeing the world. This in turn leads to the culminating task Santayana specifies: the rational poet must articulate a prophetic, probing, even religious perspective. Rational poetry must be philosophical poetry.

Discussing this requirement of poetry in its "higher function," Santayana seems to hold conflicting views. He says that the rational poet must "build new structures, richer, finer, fitter to the primary tendencies of our nature, truer to the ultimate possibilities of the soul." But a few pages later he claims that "the highest ideality is the comprehension of the real" and that "poetry is not at its best when it depicts a further possible experience, but when it initiates us, by feigning something which as an experience is impossible, into the meaning of the experience which we have actually had."[11] The first statement would commit Santayana to the belief that an interpretation of nature that did not accord with human ideals could not be truly rational. The second view finds greatest value in poetry that reveals what is meaningful throughout our actual experience of reality.

At other times, as I have noted, Santayana says that the mythical element of poetry is significant or truthful only as it symbolizes actual events. Because poetry is imaginative, its constructions will not lend themselves to verification. But, Santayana now insists, they will serve as truthful representations of nature, of the world in which we live, and they will not necessarily be idealistic. The rational poet must be metaphysical and even religious in some sense; but he may also be a realist and a pessimist. This conflict between the Platonic and naturalistic sides of Santayana's philosophy is strident in all his critical writing. In Chapter 6 I tried to reconcile his divergent statements, but perhaps I was too sanguine about their reconcilability.

It is because he thinks poetry in its highest reaches must be philosophic or religious that Santayana criticizes Shakespeare as he does. He sees him as a Renaissance man who felt he had to choose between Christianity and nothing, and who chose nothing. Denying that either religious sentiments or a philosophical scheme are to be found in Shakespeare's work, Santayana calls him a positivist devoid of metaphysical insight. He does not doubt that Shakespeare possessed great wisdom, imaginative strength, and even dialectical ability. What he finds lacking is any "cosmic consciousness." In contrast to Homer and Dante, who had a theory of life and who saw human nature in its relations to the universe, "Shakespeare's world . . . is only the world of human society."[12] And even with regard to the experience that *Hamlet* expresses, Santayana insists that "here is no necessary human tragedy, no universal destiny or divine law."[13]

Because it passes beyond the immediate aspect of experience—if not beyond experience as a whole—the fourth level of poetry is committed to referential language in a way that the first three levels are not. It interprets our immediate experience by using essences as symbols, and it formulates an ontology that may account for the nature of experience itself. This, however, requires the kind of laborious and deliberative thinking that was reserved for intellect rather than the imagination. How then can philosophical poetry be a work of fine art? How can it even be aesthetic?

In answering these questions, Santayana points out that "if we think of philosophy as an investigation into truth, or as reasoning upon truths supposed to be discovered, there is nothing in philosophy akin to poetry." Yet philosophical poetry is possible and highly desirable, he maintains. For the *vision* of philosophy may be poetic and inventive. Though philosophical activities of investigation and reasoning are "only preparatory and servile parts, means to an end," they can terminate in a contemplative intuition of everything's value and existence. "Such contemplation is imaginative. . . . A philosopher who attains it is, for the moment, a poet; and a poet who turns his practiced and passionate imagination on the order of all things, or on anything in the light of the whole, is for that moment a philosopher."[14]

In relation to its subject matter, philosophical poetry thereby meets the basic requirement for all fine art. It does not provide information so much as yield a contemplative insight into the cosmic order. It uses the discursive parts of philosophy as material perfected by a servile art and subservient to poetry's imaginative flight.

With respect to its technique, philosophical poetry, as Santayana conceives of it, may also qualify as art. Like poetry on the other levels, it can lavish attention upon the sound of its words. In its medium it need not be inferior to other poetry. But instead of being meaningless music, it sings the melodious chords of truth-seeking vision. It is more concrete and immediate than practical communication, and more significant and penetrating than unreflective verse. Rational poetry, we are assured, "present[s] in graphic images the total efficacy of real things."[15]

Before going on to examine Santayana's standard of excellence from a slightly different point of view, we might pause here to notice how Santayana's general aesthetics affects his idea of poetry. In *Reason in Art* he argues that the demarcation between poetry and prose derives from the distinction he makes between imagination and intelligence, and between fine art and servile art. In his treatment of rational poetry, however, we can see how intimately Santayana wishes to bind poetry to prose. Rather than considering them incompatible, his entire analysis tries to show how they work together and benefit from their mutual cooperation.

By including what is visionary in philosophy, Santayana states, poetry can speak with authority about the real world. By combining philosophic interest with the purity of music in words, poetry becomes both expressive and meaningful. Santayana does not recognize any insuperable barrier between poetry and prose. But he does treat them as vastly different modes of language, one instrumental to the liberal operation of the other, one of them servile and the other fine art. Even in the close integration that he recommends, they are split by the same kind of dualism that his philosophy employs to separate immediate from mediate experience and essence from existence.

Santayana's conception of great art, more specifically great poetry, consists of three requirements: First, it must have a perfectly determinate form. The words must contribute to a highly unified pattern. The sounds must be organized according to definite rhythmic schemes. The relevant images must form a picture, or series of pictures, that is centered in itself as the unity of a manifold.

Second, great poetry must be composed of the most suitable materials. It must use sounds that are rhythmic and harmonious, words that are rich and suggestive, and images that are graphic and stimulating. But since determinate form as listed under the first requirement is uppermost in importance, the effects of euphony, euphuism, and image making must be subordinated accordingly.

Third, great poetry must express a significant world outlook. Its interpretation of both the human condition and the world in general must be valid. At the same time, the presentation of this philosophical vision must not be overly technical or discursive, and it must subserve the requirements of formal and material beauty.

These requirements may suffice for great poetry, but they cannot account for the very greatest poetry. At this point we may return, in a way that will amplify my comments in Chapter 6, to Santayana's discussion of Lucretius, Dante, and Goethe. Though these three are all philosophical poets and all great poets, the efforts of each are treated as imperfect and in need of augmentation by the virtues of the others. They are great poets because they express, in beautiful and determinate form, a large and penetrating view of reality. Yet each is criticized for being limited in his outlook and unable to express the intuitions of the other two.

In Santayana's interpretation, "Goethe is the poet of life; Lucretius the poet of nature; Dante the poet of salvation."[16] Portraying experience in its immediacy, its infinite diversity, and its apparent absurdity, Goethe depicts a world that is bounded by the ego, that is constituted by human feelings or ideas. His writing tends to be subjectivistic and impressionistic. To Goethe's vision must be added that of Lucretius, whose naturalism gives him an insight into the substance of things. Though he subordinates human experience to the causes and conditions that underlie it, Lucretius has a truthful understanding of life. His finger is on the pulse of matter, and he knows the secret workings of both Venus and Mars, both genesis and destruction. But he is not especially perceptive of values. To Dante is given the knowledge of good and evil, the ideal and the anti-ideal. More than the other two, Dante understands the life of contemplation and spiritual harmony.

As I have suggested, this family portrait represents three sides of Santayana's own nature and corresponds, more or less, to the three principal categories of his philosophy. Goethe sees the foreground of essences; Lucretius understands material substance; Dante appreciates the moral and religious discipline needed for the purification of spirit. Just as essence, matter, and spirit are coordinated in a specific arrangement and interrelation, so too does Santayana place the three great poets in a hierarchical order. His "sense of what is real and important" shows him how to integrate the poetic virtues of all three. He formulates his conception of the greatest poet in accordance with this integration.

Even though Santayana places Goethe at the bottom and Dante at the top of this hierarchy, he knows that what counts is more than just the level on which a poet travels. What the poet brings into that level is also important. Santayana recognizes that Goethe on the lowest rung has a kind of awareness one does not find in either Lucretius or Dante. Goethe reveals the variegated plenitude of life, the "magical medley . . . of images, passions, memories, and introspective wisdom that Lucretius could not have dreamed of." Lucretius in turn is more sane and rational than Dante, whose supernatural views are childish. Dante's idea of nature "is not genuine; it is not sincerely put together out of reasoned observation."[17] It is egocentric and anthropomorphic. It envisages man as the center of the universe and takes the mirror of his purposive and teleological nature to be a window into the world.

In resembling Dante, Shelley also appreciates the moral and spiritual aspirations of human nature, its contemplative upper half. But Shelley, too, is limited by an "obtuseness to things dynamic—to the material order." Yet Santayana insists that the principles to which Shelley and Dante appeal are needed for a true representation of human nature: "They are good principles for fiction, for poetry, for morals, for religion."[18] Shelley achieves purity of thought and expression; Dante's powers of idealization enable him to touch "the ultimate goal to which a poet can aspire."[19]

In harmonizing the three different perspectives, the ideal poet does not neglect the goodness of each level. But he is thought to arrange them in the hierarchy Santayana prescribes. Thus, just as he usually takes idealization to be the most aesthetic element, and just as his idea of rational poetry emphasizes the manifestation of norms or moral goals, rather than a merely realistic portrayal of nature, here too Santayana favors the presentation of an ideal. Though the greatest poet will accommodate the textural wealth of experiences and recognize the nonpurposive character of the physical world, all this must lead up to a vision of the good and a contemplation of perfection.

Santayana was fully cognizant of the difficulties in uniting such contrasting approaches. But he claims it can be done: "This union is not impossible." For it to occur, rational art must be in harmony with activities that buttress life—industry, science, business, morality, politics, social action. The resulting unity provides an aesthetic element to all experience, and everything we do becomes a work of art. In this respect "the philosophical or comprehensive poet, like Homer, like Shakespeare, would be a poet of business." Still, work and business are not enough; the greatest poet has a higher responsibility. He must express "the ideal towards which we would move under . . . improved conditions." This ideal includes the art of playing well, in addition to working well. It is based on the art of purposive life but far transcends it in the direction of spiritual liberation. That is the ultimate end of the greatest poet, who will, however, succeed in the practical sphere as well, joining and refining both dimensions. Of him one may truly say: "*Onorate l'altissimo poeta.* Honour the most high poet, honour the highest possible poet. But this supreme poet is in limbo still."[20]

That statement is not, however, Santayana's final word. Eleven years after *Three Philosophical Poets* appeared, he published the article "On My Friendly Critics." In it Santayana devotes only one paragraph to his current thinking about the standard of excellence in poetry. In an attempt to see how Santayana's earlier and later views are related to each other, I quote again the most pertinent lines in that paragraph: "So anxious was I, when younger, to find some rational justification for poetry and religion [that] . . . I maintained that the noblest poetry also must express the moral burden of life and must be rich in wisdom. Age has made me less exacting, and I can now find quite sufficient perfection in poetry . . . without much philosophic scope . . . if it utters the vital impulses of that moment with enough completeness [and there is] an adequate expression of the soul. . . . To be poetical or religious intrinsically, the mystic cry is enough."[21]

This passage could be taken to mean that what is "intrinsically" poetic—that is, coherent with the mere definition of poetry—need not include expression or representation. But this much Santayana had always maintained. There would have been no occasion for him to change a previous position. In view of the fact that he talks about "the noblest poetry," I think he wanted to revise his former standard of poetic excellence. He had come to believe that although philosophical poetry is more than just a lyric cry it need not be considered greater or more nearly perfect than less ambitious poetry. If that is what Santayana did mean, his subsequent view differs greatly from his characteristic position in *Reason in Art*. There he says that "the noblest art will be the one, whether plastic or literary or dialectical, which creates figments most truly representative of what is momentous in human life."[22] It would seem, then, that his two standards of excellence are distinctly incompatible.

Santayana's first standard, culminating in his description of the greatest poet, was conceived during the period before 1910 when he was exploring the life of reason. His orientation at that time is marked by an optimistic and affirmative belief in magnificent harmonizations. The standard he enunciates is very strict and his ideal of *l'altissimo* quite remote. The second standard, which denies that the noblest poetry need "express the moral burden of life" or be rich in wisdom, fits in well with the older Santayana's increased sympathy with a life of sheer contemplation. Where the earlier standard employs the notion of harmony as a rationalizing influence imposed upon divergent interests, the later standard treats harmony as the focus or inward integration that essence inherently presupposes. The earlier standard includes the requirements of determinate form and suitable materials, but it exceeds them in demanding an outlook in which a truthful understanding of the world is subordinate to a search for ideals. The second standard, denying that philosophical scope is necessary, defines the noblest art in terms of "adequacy" and "completeness." The bird song is deemed infinitely rich if "it utters the vital impulses of that moment with enough completeness." It need only have "lyric adequacy" and be an "adequate expression of the soul."[23]

Just as we must wonder what makes an interest "harmonious" or "perfect" or "inwardly integrated," so too must we ask what renders a work of art "adequate" or "complete" apart from any practical wisdom or philosophical truth that it expresses. Santayana considers an interest to be harmonious or perfect if it embodies a contemplated essence. Similarly, an artwork satisfies his later standard of excellence if it unites the simple or complex essences of suitable materials and determinate form, regardless of how much or how little philosophical scope it might also have. Santayana's later standard limits itself to the first and second requirements of his earlier standard. We may, therefore, find it profitable to examine the later standard before moving on to the additional requirements that are involved in the earlier one.

According to Santayana, the only kind of form that can be worthy of great art is what he calls "typical form." It alone presents a complex essence freed of all extraneous relations. It organizes materials into a perfectly determinate pattern—a unity that is simple, idealized, satisfying, and precise in a way that neither indeterminate nor overly determinate (discursive) forms can be. But Santayana may have erred in this assumption. I will argue that what he calls either indeterminate or overly determinate form can be as definite and clear-cut as the ones that he prefers, and that none of these is necessarily more aesthetic than any other.

Santayana's theory is based on his belief that form can be disintegrated into material components. He claims that when this happens—for instance, in the paintings of the impressionists—one encounters forms that are indeterminate. In such paintings, he says, spectators must unify the given materials themselves, by means of their own interpretative faculties. What Santayana overlooks is the fact that materials are always perceived in *some* organization. Otherwise they could not be seen even as materials. Furthermore, the perception of form need not be explained in terms of essences, and when it is not, all of painting—impressionism included—can be said to depend on interpretation of one sort or another. To that extent Santayana's criticism of the impressionists, and of more recent artists who employ what he would condemn as indeterminate form, is ill-founded from the very start.

As against Santayana's view, one might argue that the impressionists do not present sense-data that the observer is expected to make into a perceptual object. They do not appeal to the spectator's interpretative faculties any more than other artists. They do not proffer uninterpreted essences, and neither do they restrict themselves to materials without determinate form. Instead, they paint a scene as it appears to them under the special conditions coherent with their individual modes of interpretation. Monet's haystacks are not the materials or simple essences out of which the spectator is supposed to construct anything. They represent haystacks in the world that look this way at different positions of the sun, and as they are perceived by the artist. Later on, the paintings of the impressionists became more and more abstract. But this does not mean that they stripped away artistic interpretation. It only signifies that they avoided iconic or literal representation, and therefore that spectators who seek exact likenesses are looking for the wrong thing. Throughout their historical development, the impressionists used forms that not only organize colors in determinate patterns but also express visual meanings these painters could not have conveyed otherwise.

At the opposite extreme, Santayana's antipathy toward discursive or "overly-determinate" form seems to be a dislike of highly elaborate structures. He is surely justified in stressing the need for selection. The artist who dazzles the spectators with a succession of increasingly complicated details may cause them to lose sight of the total unity in which these details are supposed to fit. But a priori there is no reason to think that an intricate pattern cannot be satisfying or harmonious. It became fashionable in the twentieth century to prefer streamlined shapes rather than heavily laden ornaments. But ours is a self-conscious age that can easily feel embarrassed by elegant diversity and lavish figuration. When a discursive form seems unimaginative or dull, it ought to be sacrificed in favor of simplicity. But the same should be said about simplicity, which often lacks richness and variety. From this, it does not follow that one can exclude even the most discursive forms merely because of their inherent complexity.

Furthermore, Santayana's belief that the most desirable form is typical form gives too much preference to idealization at the expense of realistic representation. At times, Santayana seems to mean that typical form provides something that has general appeal, something that is easily recognized to be "true to" life, typical in the sense of being universal or pervasive. But if this is what Santayana means, why does he think that the use of typical form must eschew realistic interpretation? To see something as being true to life is to see it in terms of a great number of actual facts, and by means of a process that evaluates the object's cognitive and affective function in reality. Judged to be aesthetically truthful, a presentation becomes more determinate for consciousness than it was before. Having passed through this mediating experience of art, it is anything but a bare or directly given essence.

Santayana tends to think that the best forms are those that are tightly organized and follow rigid conventions. Against "romantic formlessness" he pits "classical unity." In making his judgment, Santayana does not seem to be expressing a mere preference. He does not appear to be choosing the sonnet form, let us say, rather than *vers libre* simply as a matter of personal taste. On the contrary, he is distinguishing an inherently better or more beautiful form from one that is inevitably worse. But is his position defensible? I do not think so.

For one thing, there is no way of deciding beforehand what pattern, organization, technique, or type of unity will be most suitable for a work of art. Much Romantic art succeeds precisely because it escapes the constraints of a regular, highly demarcated pattern. And though an artist can always benefit from the use of traditional forms, he will not make a completely satisfying product unless he manipulates these forms in keeping with his own artistic needs. In relation to some materials a form may be inappropriate although it is eminently suitable with others. In relation to some forms a particular type of representation may be ill-advised, though entirely correct for others.

No standard forms, materials, or modes of representation can be ordained as necessarily best in all circumstances. The artist must rely on his or her intelligence and imagination in order to decide. The critic, assessing an artistic object on the basis of its total aesthetic merit, must realize that each of the components can be evaluated only by reference to its utility for this particular work of art. Without that unbiased and pluralistic attitude, no critical evaluation can be judicious. Whether the artist *ought* to make just this presentation of aesthetic effects and not another is a moral or quasi-moral problem of a different sort. I will consider it in Chapter 8.

We may now return to Santayana's first standard, which differs from his second in requiring philosophic scope and prophetic insight. Since both of these requirements must be subordinate to the ideal of typical form, the core of the two standards remains the same. The later Santayana just sloughs off the further requirements of the earlier one.

However desirable Santayana's initial insistence upon philosophic scope may or may not be, one might construe his fundamental concept more broadly than he does. Santayana seems to believe that a poet cannot be philosophical unless he or she puts into verse a fully developed metaphysical system. With this as the ruling criterion, a poet like Shakespeare does not fare too well. Still, as we have seen, Santayana himself praises Shakespeare for expressing a great deal of wisdom, and in the same volume in which he denies that Shakespeare has a religion he uses him as the shattering contrast to Browning: "Shakespeare, without being especially a philosopher, stands by virtue of his superlative genius on the plane of universal reason, far above the passionate experience which he overlooks and on which he reflects; and he raises us for the moment to his level, to send us back again, if not better endowed for practical life, at least not unacquainted with speculation."[24] But despite his "superlative genius on the plane of universal reason," Shakespeare is not credited with any philosophic scope.

We can certainly agree that Shakespeare is not a philosopher comparable to Dante, Goethe, Lucretius, or Shelley. Nevertheless,

I wonder whether a distinction cannot be made between a philosophical poet, in the sense that Santayana prescribes, and a poet who has philosophic scope. The latter has a comprehensive world outlook as well as an understanding of human nature regardless of the fact that he or she might be lacking as a philosopher or theologian.

Shakespeare was untroubled by religious or metaphysical problems not because he was insensitive to them, but only because he was more concerned about moral issues. Questions of purpose, justifiable conduct, and significant social intercourse were, for him, most important. Hamlet holds religious beliefs and voices them on occasion, and so does Macbeth; but the dimensions of life that confront Hamlet and Macbeth in each play do not themselves pertain to religion. Hamlet's desperation is caused by his inability to act reflectively or even to decide whether a life of uncertainty is worth living; Macbeth's progressive misery results from his miscalculation about the changes in his psychological fortitude that would result from murdering Duncan and Banquo.

In this connection, it is interesting to note that, as an illustration of how Shakespeare depicts life "without a meaning," Santayana quotes the lines of Macbeth that begin "To-morrow, and to-morrow, and to-morrow." But these lines are not a statement of Shakespeare's own philosophy; they are the words of a wretched, half-crazed Macbeth whose repudiation of meaning in life reveals the depths to which his behavior has carried him. The speech is itself a "correlative object" for Macbeth's predicament, and Shakespeare's capacity to use it as such reveals his greatness not only as a dramatist but also as a thinker. In "Tragic Philosophy," Santayana quotes Macbeth's lines again and this time denies that Shakespeare was thereby expressing his own "settled doctrine." All the same, Santayana repeats his earlier belief that Shakespeare had no philosophic scope: "Even in a Hamlet, a Prospero or a Jaques, in a Henry VI or an Isabella, the poet feels no inner loyalty to the convictions he rehearses; they are like the cap and bells of his fools; and possibly if he had been pressed by some tiresome friend to propound a personal philosophy, he might have found in his irritation nothing else to fall back upon than the animal despair of Macbeth."[25]

In rejecting this approach, we may well insist that poets like Shakespeare need not be said to lack a profound or philosophic vision of the world. A comprehensive understanding of life, enriched by the capacity to sympathize with its human and other inhabitants, is enough. Highly refined analytic powers, or even a detailed interest in the problems of philosophy, are not required.

This cuts both ways. It enables us to question Santayana's early standard because of its insistence upon religious or quasi-religious poetry. But it also shows that his later standard is confused in its conception of what is needed for "the noblest poetry." Once we recognize that form cannot be dissociated from cognitive content, we see that any "adequate expression of the soul" must also presuppose a veridical interpretation, or at least a coherent world outlook. How else can a work of art present a mature and reasoned view of life? How else can it portray humanity's place in nature?

The justification for philosophic scope in poetry issues from the fact that a work that has it can provide a vast network of intense and varied aesthetic effects. But though philosophic scope is needed for great art, it is not sufficient by itself. "Mere grace and feeling and music and cloud-castles and frolic" are good things, too, just as Santayana says. Their contribution to the greatest art is important, and we must not forget them when we come to a final reckoning.

In conclusion, I should address a difficulty that haunts Santayana's earlier standard. When he insists that the greatest poetry must be prophetic and visionary, Santayana sometimes seems to mean that it will convey deep truths, and sometimes that it will show the importance of moral and spiritual ends. The first endeavor belongs to realism; the second to idealism. By putting Dante at the head of his hierarchy, Santayana appears to favor—once again—the idealistic over the realistic.

Whatever Santayana may believe, we should not expect all of the greatest works of art to tend in either one or the other direction. And in any event, the chasm between the realistic and the idealistic is not unbridgeable. A realistic work that has philosophic scope will recognize ideals that govern daily moral choice; conversely, an idealistic work will have to show that its cherished goals are grounded in actual conditions. When idealistic art is shallow in its comprehension of life, it becomes fanciful or sentimental, or just irrelevant. When realistic art is insensitive to values, it ignores an essential part of human existence and cannot be truly philosophical.

Apart from these considerations, I fail to see how preferment can be given to works of art that either do or do not advance ideals. All artists have a right to propagandize and even to recommend political action. If they did not speak from the heart and promote what feels to them as ethically imperative, they could not make an adequate expression; their work could not be authentic or fully aesthetic. On the other hand, if they merely wish to paint a realistic picture, the job will be botched once they are forced to raise a banner. The greatest art may be realistic or idealistic, and possibly both at different times or even simultaneously in different ways. The two possibilities need not exclude each other.[26]

8   The Basis of Aesthetic and Moral Criticism

SANTAYANA'S AESTHETIC and moral philosophy culminates in a theory of criticism. Taking issue with Croce's view that aesthetics is a separate and unique science, Santayana denies that it is a science at all. In the place of an aesthetic science he finds "the art and function of criticism." By criticism Santayana means "a reasoned appreciation of human works by a mind not wholly ignorant of their subject or occasion, their school, and their process of manufacture."[1] Because a work of art is an object that enters into a variety of relations, the critic cannot limit his assessment to an evaluation of beauty. He must be a moral critic, even a moral philosopher, who helps to determine the role that an art object should play in human experience.

❋

With respect to judgments about what is or is not beautiful, Santayana denies that the critic can appeal to any quality of beauty or aesthetic excellence that would necessarily be recognized by all other observers. He denies that aesthetic judgments can have a universal application, and he constantly reminds us that uniform agreement in particular evaluations does not exist. He claims that any resemblance between critical opinions depends on the similar "origin, nature, and circumstance" of the critics themselves. "It is unmeaning to say that what is beautiful to one man *ought* to be beautiful to another. If their senses are the same, their associations and dispositions similar, then the same thing will certainly be beautiful to both. . . . But no two men have exactly the same faculties, nor can things have for any two exactly the same values."[2]

The desire to attain agreement about aesthetic value Santayana considers to be dogmatism, or insecurity, or just a lack of sensibility. People who *know* what is fine do not wish to impress someone else with the rightness of their choice. They realize that appreciations will differ. Feeling no need to change the enjoyments of either themselves or those who disagree with them, they are secure within their own taste.

Still, Santayana does not want to question the possibility of an authoritative critical judgment. Although he denies there is any universal standard of excellence applicable to works of art, he suggests that "the true test is the degree and kind of satisfaction it can give to him who appreciates it most."[3] And it is obvious that by "appreciates" he here means "is responsive to" or "understands." What matters, then, is the degree and kind of satisfaction available to a discriminating critic.

When Santayana discusses the "criterion of taste," he lays great emphasis upon the amount and type of satisfaction. Santayana takes a criterion of taste to be a guide to what delights us, how our aesthetic experience is conditioned by our nature and our interests, the kind of enjoyment that others have and that may be possible for us, and finally, the way in which an object that pleases us may or may not be harmonized with the rest of our interests. In describing the criterion of taste, he mentions three subordinate principles and outlines a natural history of "good taste."

Taste that is good originally occurs in moments when "aesthetic emotion is massive and distinct." Our ability to decide, to know what is worthy of our choice, is initially dependent upon some stirring experience that we have had in the presence of an object. What usually matters most is the amount of satisfaction and the ultimacy of "vital over verbal judgments." But although it is the "volume and intensity" of our own experience that determines what we shall henceforth choose, the ability to discriminate may be acquired under tutelage. Having been introduced to the beauties of art and nature by one who nurtured our appreciation through the example of his or her superior enjoyment, we tend to treat the tutor's judgments as the norm, for they were "the source and exemplar of all our own."[4] We take this person's degree of satisfaction to be the criterion, and we do not (it would appear) restrict our response to the "vital judgments" that we have made ourselves. What our tutor has felt, even if we have not, helps us decide what is really good. How Santayana would distinguish a judgment based on the tutor's experience from a "verbal judgment" I cannot tell.

Though dependent on the volume and intensity of appreciation, good taste includes much more. A vivid feeling may be "inwardly confused or outwardly confusing." Santayana identifies the former with inherent discords that exist when "elaborate things are attempted without enough art and refinement." Such efforts are in bad taste because they lack purity and simplicity, whether or not they stimulate great enjoyment. The virtues of purity, simplicity, inner perfection, clarity, articulateness, etc. are possessed by "wildflowers, plain chant, or a scarlet uniform."[5] These may be too simple to have a major role in the life of reason—they may have to be subordinated to other things—but in themselves, as "natural joys" and "elementary beauties," they have undoubted dignity and worth.

At its highest reach, good taste detects an object's moral significance, related to its importance for other people and other possibilities of goodness. On this level, good taste directs us toward objects that are "outwardly fit" as well as inwardly pure. Our aesthetic appreciations cannot stand by themselves. They must be compared with other enjoyments that may be available in these or similar conditions. However perfect an interest may be in itself, it can always be harmful to other interests—just as two contiguous paintings may ruin the effect that each would have if they were put in different rooms. Good taste requires the harmonization of interests. That is why the criterion of taste must include a social and moral standard. The critic must evaluate an aesthetic object in terms of its pertinence for different recipients, the width of its appeal, its capacity to serve humanity, and its general suitability under the circumstances. The life of reason demands a concern about the consequences of art as well as its inner integrity, and good taste "cannot abstract from tradition, utility, and the temper of the world."[6]

Correspondingly, Santayana insists that the critic must be ethically attuned and not just a person who is sensitive to beauty. Any occurrence of beauty may itself be criticized, and aesthetic value is always subject to moral censure. Trying to justify the existence of art, Santayana begins by pointing out that, on the whole, it is innocent. "Now art, more than any other considerable pursuit, more even than speculation, is abstract and inconsequential." Art may give expression to social changes long after their occurrence, but it is unlikely to cause them. Similarly, art "registers passions without stimulating them."[7] The artist who deals with sexual or religious subjects will not create a lascivious or pious product, but rather a work of beauty. "In so far as he is an artist in truth," he or she will make something that gives expression to erotic and devotional interests without promoting the kind of action that would satisfy them. Art is "liberal": in being aesthetic, the enjoyment it engenders is freely bestowed and intrinsically good.

As Santayana sees it, art is a typical and symbolic example of "perfect activity." It is "a rehearsal of rational living, and recasts in idea a world which we have no present means of recasting in reality." Art thereby shows the practical world what it can make of itself. Because art lives in imagination only, it cannot create this better world; but aside from the fact that practical life always employs aesthetic figments as a blueprint, art finds its rationale elsewhere. "What nature does with existence, art does with appearance."[8]

In this fashion, Santayana gives a justification for the sheer existence of art. He suggests that Plato overemphasized the influence of arts such as poetry, taking the Homeric stories too seriously and failing to realize that "left to themselves they float in an ineffectual stratum of the brain."[9] Nevertheless, Santayana approves of Plato's intentions. For Plato was specifically concerned with the criterion of taste as an agency of morality. He saw the necessity for judging appreciations ethically; and to this extent Santayana agrees with him.

Furthermore, Santayana claims that an interest in art, like an interest in the aesthetic quality of experience, ought to be harmonized with other types of life. Too frequently, art becomes an indulgence and an impediment. The involvement in artistic pursuits that either an observer or a creator may have can often separate that individual from the workaday world of honest, though routine and uninspired, endeavor. Santayana points out that such a person may become a dilettante or a virtuoso, but that he or she is unlikely to be a complete, intelligent, and happy human being. Artists are basically craftsmen, and they should find their home in the midst of society, not on its bohemian fringes or in some remote empyrean. A dedication to art should be a crowning completion in useful practice. But although art must be harmonized with industry or science, its own function is supreme: "In industry man is still servile, preparing the materials he is to use in action. . . . In science he is an observer, preparing himself for action in another way, by studying its results and conditions. But in art he is at once competent and free; he is creative."[10]

Santayana holds comparable views about the work of art itself. An aesthetic object that has no usefulness in practical, everyday living is a "baseless artifice." Instead of being socially significant, it becomes artificial and esoteric. It is usage that makes works of art most attractive and gives them their "highest expression." Art that is incapable of having practical relevance tends to be ephemeral and slight: "There has never been any art worthy of notice without a practical basis and occasion, or without some intellectual or religious function."[11] For instance, "architecture may be useful, sculpture commemorative, poetry reflective, even music, by its expression, religious or martial."[12] In a rational society works of art would be functional, and functional objects would be works of art. Applied arts would not be isolated from fine arts, nor pragmatic goods from those that are aesthetic. But although the arts would then be harmonized and coordinated so that particular objects can be both fine and useful, the distinction between useful art and fine art is one that Santayana retains. Only fine arts are devoted to what is distinctively aesthetic, and therefore only they are "ideal."

Santayana's theory of criticism merges in this manner with his conception of the good life. He says that criticism and the criterion of taste must organize our multiple interests "with a view to attaining the greatest satisfactions of which our nature is capable." But no judgment can cause a species or an individual to change its underlying constitution. Morality and good taste can only make recommendations about the perfection of one's being, the fulfillment of one's innate capacities: "All that morality can require is the inward harmony of each life."[13] In its ultimate reach, good taste endows one's total experience with the purity and integrity that spirit always seeks. When the effort succeeds, a person's life possesses the ideality of determinate form and harmonious unity.

In order to clarify Santayana's ideas about art criticism, we have to examine his general theory of morality at some length. It is there that we can best discover what he means by the word *harmony*. Santayana uses the term in two different ways. Sometimes it signifies the condition of interests that have been made mutually compatible through the mediating operation of reason or intelligence. In this regard Santayana even considers an interest in harmony itself to be a prerequisite for the life of reason. At other times, however, he employs the word to mean inward integration within a single interest, which he calls the "condition of any specific perfection." Harmony of this sort is essential not for the life of reason but for "precision in interest or passion itself."[14]

Though Santayana sometimes employs *harmony* in one sense and sometimes in the other, his discussion of intrinsic value usually relies on the second sense. With respect to morality as a whole, however, the fact that Santayana has two different concepts of harmony poses a major difficulty. It was the "relativity of morals" that Santayana claimed to be defending when he made explicit the second meaning. And yet he had previously devoted *The Life of Reason* to the elaborate exposition of what harmony, in its first signification, would require. To many readers it seemed obvious that harmony, as the ideal of a life of reason, was the universal standard that Santayana recommended. How then can he reconcile these different conceptions of harmony?

This kind of problem appears several times in the polemical exchange between Santayana and his critics in the Schilpp volume devoted to his philosophy. The arguments that Eliseo Vivas, Irwin Edman, and Milton Karl Munitz there present turn on the supposed conflict between Santayana's earlier and later philosophy. In his earlier work, Santayana is understood to have advocated a standard of intelligence as the means of determining what would be an "objectively moral act" under specified circumstances—that is, an act that might be justified for all persons similarly situated. In his later philosophy Santayana is thought to have renounced the ideal of intelligence and substituted an interest in contemplated essences, an interest that is accepted and approved not because it harmonizes best with other interests but because it is one in which purity, precision, and perfection are uniquely revealed. In his book on Santayana's moral philosophy, Munitz states the critical position as follows: "Santayana has described the spiritual life in two opposite and incompatible ways: on the one hand, as a life of understanding, in which cognitive intent . . . is directed upon the ideals of truth and clarity of meaning; and on the other, as an escape from existence, as a disintoxication from all ideals, as a reversion to the immediately given that in itself possesses no meaning or significance."[15]

Like the other critics, Munitz holds that Santayana's later philosophy, with its recurrent reference to spirituality, offers a second moral standard that is both contradictory and inferior to his former criterion of harmony through reason. Santayana's response, in "Apologia Pro Mente Sua," resolves the difficulty that disturbed his critics, although, as I will show later on, his explanation poses further problems. In his reply Santayana appeals to the relativity of morals in a new context. Moral relativity, he says, considers all interests intrinsically valuable if only they are inwardly integrated, but it also demands that the choice between a perfect passion that does not harmonize with our other interests and one, perhaps less attractive, that does harmonize must be left to the person who has to choose. People should do what it is in their individual nature to do; the life of reason may be good for some persons, but for others it may be detrimental to their ultimate destiny. And the same, he asserts, is true of spirituality.

This kind of relativism had occurred in many of Santayana's works. But it was often accompanied by statements that *seemed* to advocate, as objective and dogmatic standards, first the life of reason and later the life of pure spirit. The following quotations give some of his clearer utterances about moral relativity:

> It is prudent to be rational up to a certain point, because if we neglect too many or too deeply rooted impulses in ourselves or in the world, our master-passion itself will come to grief; but too much rationality might be fatal to that passion at once. . . . The impulse to be rational and to establish harmony in oneself and in the world may be itself a "higher" impulse than others, in that it presupposes them; yet the romantic impulse to be rash, or the sudden call to be converted, might be thought "higher" than rationality by many people. Reason alone can be rational, but it does not follow that reason alone is good. The criterion of worth remains always the voice of nature, truly consulted, in the person that speaks.
>
> Spirituality is the supreme good for those who are called to it. . . . Just as the value of an artist must be judged by the

world, in view of all the interests which his art affects or subserves, while the artist himself lives only in his own labour, irresponsible, technical, and visionary; so the value of spiritual life in general . . . must be judged morally by the world, in view of its own ambitions, while the spirit judges the world and its ambitions spiritually.

[With reference to the contemplation of essences:] Is it *better* to do this than not to do it? It is certainly better if you are committed to that task, or love that employment; but if you ask me whether it is better to be so committed, or so to love, I am speechless. Is it better to live than not to live? . . . My own feeling rather prompts me to think life and to think contemplation and to think riches a good when they come spontaneously, and an evil when they are constrained or distracted; but this is only a way of avoiding the question, and leaving it to each spirit at each moment to judge for itself. I am not a dogmatist in ethics.[16]

If Santayana is not a dogmatist in ethics, he cannot maintain *any* objective moral standard. As a moral relativist, he can make no judgments about what other people ought to do. How, then, are we to interpret his earlier defense of the life of reason and his later concern for the contemplation of essences? I think that they should be taken more as expressions of Santayana's own personal inclinations than as theoretical or doctrinal positions in ethics. Throughout his life Santayana's dedication to reason remained constant. That is why he said he frankly cleaves to the Greeks and not the Indians, aspiring to be a rational animal and not a pure spirit. He did not waver in his belief that the barbarian, controlled by his master-passion, does not think about the consequences of submitting to it, and therefore acts in lamentable ignorance.

Unhampered by any knowledge of himself, the person Santayana calls barbaric succumbs to the Romantic impulse of being rash. To ask such people to consider whether they have properly consulted the voice of their own nature is to ask them not to be barbarians. Like his pragmatist critics, Santayana consistently makes this demand. Both early and late in his philosophy, he extols the ability to assess and criticize one's master-passion; and that can be done only by a genuine and careful reliance upon rationality and intelligence.

Therefore I do not agree with critics of Santayana who complain that his later philosophy relinquished the objective standard of reason. In the only sense in which he maintained that standard as a young man, he also did so as an older one. Like the pragmatists, he was, in all his writing, a relativist insofar as he denied that any judge or observer can determine a priori which kind of life is objectively best for another person. At the same time, he maintained that people can reach a valid decision about themselves if they harken to "the voice of nature" and adhere to veridical insights about what they are as just the individuals they happen to be.

This combination of relativity and concern for objective truth in moral matters may be adequate for the purposes at hand. Still, we may wonder how one can attain the veridical insights Santayana demands. Is there a supervening criterion or decision procedure that would enable us to sort out the true and false statements about someone's "real nature"?

According to Santayana, and John Dewey as well, the good life for a human being is any life that truly harmonizes the various interests and passions of that particular person. But the meaning of *harmony* still remains unclear. As the word is ordinarily used, one might well say that every interest can be harmonized, somehow or other, with an indefinite number of other interests. Yet neither Santayana nor Dewey would treat all interests as equally desirable. They would insist that most of them are not truly harmonious, that most of them do not accord with one's real nature. But how are we to know wherein true harmony consists? How are we to decide that one way of life is better or more harmonious than another?

In *Dominations and Powers* Santayana makes his most thorough attempt to grapple with this issue. There he says: "Primal Will and Circumstances, not the man's wishes or the reformer's prescription, determine the true interests of each person. And this is also the criterion by which the genius or folly of the directive imagination would be determined." By primal Will in man Santayana means the complexity of primitive needs and impulses that motivate psyche to exploration and activity, even though the organism does not know what it wants or what would satisfy its need. We cannot stop here to examine Santayana's position fully, but we should notice how he defines Will: "the universal movement of nature, even if quite unconscious, in so far as running through a cycle or trope it precipitates a result that seems to us a consummation."[17]

In Santayana's opinion, Will is blind and unreasoning in itself. It must be ruled by intelligence, and the rational justification of any volitional act stems from the likelihood of achieving practical success. "That which makes an action rational is the material possibility of carrying it out successfully. In a word, *Circumstances* render one action rational and another irrational." No impulse is intrinsically right, Santayana now maintains, and none is intrinsically wrong, except in relation to its suitability in the actual world. "You have a right to be what you are and to become what you can become."[18]

This combination of primal Will and suitability under the circumstances Santayana offers as the objective standard of moral value. He explicitly rejects, as I think he always had, any relativity of morals that denies that true and justifiable statements about one's nature can be made. Authoritative judgments disclose the rational rightness of one act or impulse rather than another, and this depends on feasibility under the actual conditions. Santayana goes on to admit that in a sense his position supports the maxim that Might is Right. On his view, any successful act is right. At the same time, he insists that his doctrine is in fact more intricate: for the man who believes that Might is Right will land himself in moral contradictions if he thinks that sheer license pays off. Such a person "may always do as he likes, but he will seldom get what he wants. He will prove himself a fool, in little things and in great, if he persistently pursues what Circumstances deny him."[19]

This seems to be Santayana's clearest statement of his ethical views. It closely resembles the pragmatist emphasis upon the moral importance of opportune acts and the necessity for considering the consequences of one's behavior. But toward Santayana and the pragmatists alike I must still direct one final question. What is the criterion for choosing among interests or impulses all of which are feasible under the circumstances and capable of being carried out successfully? Of two or more interests that might be suitable, which should we choose?

Neither Santayana nor Dewey answers this kind of question. I once tried to show that Dewey's theory of value (as well as his ethical and political philosophy, which also claims that objective goods can be discovered solely by means of a critical method that judges the consequences of an act and its feasibility under the circumstances) presupposes unexamined standards that determine the way in which a decision is to be made. Assuming that an indefinite number of different interests could be satisfied under most circumstances, and would therefore fit into some harmonious system or other, I argued that Dewey's a priori standards allowed only a few interests to be morally or objectively acceptable under *any* circumstances. I did not, and do not, claim that presuppositions of this sort are undesirable, or that Dewey's are repugnant, but only that his method of deciding what is and is not objectively valuable is based on criteria of which he did not seem to be aware. I concluded that the very existence of these criteria makes it impossible for objective values to be discovered simply by evaluating circumstances.[20]

Something similar can be said about Santayana's ethical and political philosophy. Bertrand Russell presents an argument to that effect in the Schilpp volume on Santayana. Russell remarks that Santayana's *The Life of Reason* pretends to define rational conduct solely in terms of harmonization of interests but in fact assumes the preferability of whatever supports a cultivated and aristocratic society. Russell maintains that Santayana's ethical statements "imply that culture is to be sought even at the cost of a vast accumulation of human suffering."[21]

Regardless of what Santayana's presuppositions may be, I suggest that apart from these implied standards his official theory, like Dewey's, does not yield a basis for choosing among all the varied interests that could be carried out successfully on some occasion. And this, I believe, is a serious shortcoming. For Santayana's ethical theory cannot really meet the arguments of one who believes that Might makes Right. The person with sufficient might will alter the circumstances according to his own designs. Then anything he desires will be attainable, and hence, on Santayana's theory, morally justified. Santayana might continue to deny that such a person, doing what he likes, gets "what he wants." But circumstances are arranged so that he does get what he wants. Santayana might reply that the individual does not get what he *really* wants. Yet Santayana has also told us that primal Will and Circumstances determine the "true interest of each person." If Santayana were consistent, he would have to applaud every domination and become a universal camp follower.

The dilemma in which Santayana and the pragmatists find themselves, required to treat every successful act as morally justifiable or else to presuppose some ethical standard that manages to put them on the side of the angels after all, is eliminated once we realize that neither primal Will nor Circumstances can indicate where one's true interests lie. Both needs and the situations in which they arise are subject to change. At times people sacrifice their interests rather than try to resist circumstances that are inimical to any satisfying completion. At other times, however, men and women may put primal Will first and do everything in their power to mold the circumstances accordingly. The moral situation is always fluid. Individuals must know not only what they are but also what they want to make of themselves. They can try to modify their attributes, as they currently exist, or they can try to control the environment. They can succumb to an impulse that may succeed under the circumstances, or they can choose one that may possibly win out in a more favorable environment. But which choice *should* they make?

To this kind of question there is no single valid answer. With the pragmatists we must insist that antecedent to, and apart from each moral situation no one can justifiably recommend that someone change either himself or the circumstances. Having said this, however, we must also recognize that a person who is not completely stymied by the alternatives will rely on *some* prior standard in order to be able to resolve the dilemma and choose at all. And are we ourselves not presupposing some such standard when we state the conditions for a "justifiable" recommendation? What, then, is this standard?

One possible reply, often given in twentieth-century philosophy, is related to the idea that intrinsic value must ultimately depend on what is satisfying to some individual. In a problematic situation we are forced to choose between different values: between the satisfaction that would result from changing ourselves and the satisfaction that would result from changing the world. What we ought to choose, one might say, is any action that provides the greater amount of satisfaction. To this extent, the fundamental standard is quantitative, ideality pertaining to whatever is likely to be most consummatory. We frequently forgo intense satisfactions, but usually because of their distasteful consequences; and if we choose a lesser satisfaction, we generally do so because it conduces to future experience that will harmonize, we hope, the greatest consummation that is possible. Harmonization itself we may define as any satisfying coordination.

Still, a purely quantitative standard is not enough. Although we may agree that a life of greater consummation is better than a life of lesser consummation, we may not believe that a life of constant exhilaration is more desirable than a calmer, less ebullient, one. Which truly constitutes the good life? Until we can specify the qualitative aspect of our choice, we cannot claim to have given an acceptable standard of morality.

Before suggesting a solution, I want to return to Santayana's theories about the nature of criticism and the criterion of taste. The reader may already feel that our digression has carried us too far afield. By means of it, however, we are now in a position to understand Santayana's aesthetics better than we could have otherwise.[22]

Santayana's views about art criticism seem to take two different paths. On the one hand, as we saw, he claims it is unmeaning or absurd "to say that what is beautiful to one man *ought* to be beautiful to another." On the other hand, he also maintains, just two pages later, that the "true test" of what is beautiful depends on the degree and kind of satisfaction experienced by the most appreciative critic. These assertions are not contradictory in any formal sense, but they seem to pull in alternate directions. Stephen Pepper thought that Santayana's first statement might be construed to deny any "objective basis" for criticism; the second he interpreted as meaning that "a work of art of great aesthetic value is one that

affords a great deal of immediate pleasure to a highly discriminatory taste."[23]

These two approaches to aesthetic criticism can be reconciled in
the same way as Santayana's different approaches to morality. On
one level, Santayana is what may be called "a critical relativist"; on
another level, he is a "critical dogmatist." He is relativistic inasmuch
as he recognizes that differences of origin, interest, and circumstance among people cause them to find beauty in different places.
This accounts for the fact that many of the major works of one age
are boring to the next, and that even within a single age critics with
the highest awareness, intelligence, and integrity frequently differ
in their appraisals. At the same time, Santayana realizes that not everyone's opinion has "rational justification." One cannot criticize Bach
properly without having a knowledge of counterpoint.

Just as Santayana does not specify a way of life that is best for all
men and women, neither does he recommend a work of art that
everyone would or should find beautiful. But as a reasonable moral
decision is based on an intelligent evaluation of the circumstances,
so too does an adequate critical judgment depend on refined appreciation and discriminating taste. One's "true interests" are determined by primal Will and Circumstances; the "true test" of a
work of art is the degree and kind of satisfaction that it provides the
person who understands it best. The aesthetic judgments of different critics need not be the same. If they are all equally discriminating about the work at hand, however, their disagreement merely
signifies that they have different likes and dislikes and are satisfied
by different kinds of things. An objective aesthetic judgment—that
is, a valid or rationally justifiable one—would be any judgment
made by a highly discriminating critic on the basis of his or her experience. It is only in this sense, I believe, that Santayana would try
to justify his own literary criticism.

Although this interpretation of Santayana's critical theory has been pieced together from scattered statements of his, it represents the position that he mainly seemed to hold. His theory invites discussion in relation to the following questions: First, who is worthy of being treated as an authoritative or ideal critic? Second, what things ought we to enjoy, which aesthetic experiences ought we to cultivate? Santayana's desire to combine critical relativism with critical dogmatism is entirely commendable, but his philosophy of art suffers from the same methodological difficulties as his moral philosophy. Examination of each of the questions may serve to point them out. Although Santayana barely deals with these issues, his ideas about rational justification give us a starting point.

In evaluations of art, Santayana says, critical debates never end, since a critic may always appear with a "fresh temperament or a new criterion."[24] But though he recognizes that these two factors contribute to the critical situation, Santayana does not subject them to sufficient analysis. As a result, he tends to ignore the volatile and unterminated character of aesthetic experience as it normally exists. A critic's temperament, preferences, prejudices, likes and dislikes must themselves be scrutinized; and the same holds for his own "criterion," his type or degree of insight and discrimination. Not all judgments that meet Santayana's requirements are necessarily authoritative. Some of them are made by critics unduly subject to personal bias. Many sophisticated critics are scornful of religious verse, for instance, simply because they dislike the sentiments being expressed; and the recent revulsion from proletarian literature is due to a shift in global politics more than a change in the reading public's artistic comprehension.

On the other hand, even critics who are favorably disposed toward a work, or are not prejudiced against it, may be guilty of sophistication that is too narrow—too greatly based on purely technical knowledge, too often concerned about minutiae, and in general too arcane or intellectual. A critic who suffers from professional inbreeding and is so immured in his own specialty that he cannot enjoy the more commonplace and possibly less discriminating values of a work, can be as unreliable as an insensitive boor. Both offend against the standard of intelligence that is inherent in good criticism.

The ideal critic, the one whose aesthetic attitude we may take to be authoritative, would be the critic who overcomes both these drawbacks with respect to the object in question. His temperament, preferences, likes and dislikes would not be such as to prevent him from assuming an interest in this particular work or from appreciating it to the full. He would be equipped with powers of perception that open his eyes to many important values in the artistic effort without being fixated on every minor blemish. Each work requires its own kind of ideal critic. A good judge of the baroque may be inadequate for jazz, just as a good judge of music may be worthless for painting. To discover which real, live critics approximate the ideal, we would resort to the same empirical methods ordinarily used to decide whether a person is discriminating and impartial in any other field.

But what things *ought* we to enjoy and find beautiful? Although it may be true that only the judgments of ideal critics are authoritative, it is possible that in many cases we should avoid what they experience. Their judgments can have rational justification in questions of aesthetic excellence without being acceptable as recommendations about which work of art is morally preferable when compared with another. The judgments of ideal critics may inform us about artistic value, but not, necessarily, about ethical value. It is this differentiation between the aesthetic and the moral that Santayana recognizes when he adds a third principle to his criterion of excellence. The first principle requires voluminous satisfaction, and the second, inward perfection. In asking how the choices of ideal critics can be justified for other people, we move on to the principle of good taste and return to the moral issues we previously considered.

We have already seen that different ideal critics will make different recommendations. Which one should we take? As judgments about beauty or artistic value, they may all be authoritative. Works of art are neither good, bad, nor indifferent except in relation to someone's experience; but in specifying an authoritative type of aesthetic response, we never expected its individual instances to be identical in every detail. Because they are not alike, as evidenced by the diversity of conflicting but equally justifiable evaluations, we must choose among ideal critics.

This kind of choice is not a strictly aesthetic one. We are once again in the moral situation, forced to question both our personal interests and our circumstances. Our interests may tell us to retain our own established preferences or inclinations and, therefore, to emulate ideal critics who resemble us as we exist at the moment. The relevant circumstances are composed of alternate possibilities that other ideal critics find aesthetically pleasing and that we cannot currently appreciate. Shall we try to change ourselves in order to become receptive to these artistic consummations that now elude us, or shall we cultivate our garden, expending our energy on the search for more of the goodness that we can and do enjoy? Shall we stand by our present taste, or shall we sacrifice it whenever it keeps us from looking for something that may be better?

Up to a point, all such questions are only theoretical. As a matter of fact, we cannot leap out of our skins. Our likes and dislikes, as well as our general orientation in life, are largely governed by the conditions that have made us what we are. Our capacities are not unlimited, and our personal development is not entirely malleable. Nevertheless, both our preferences and our perspectives are subject to criticism. The tenets of a world outlook are mainly empirical beliefs whose cognitive warrant changes with new accretions to our conceptual equipment and experience of reality. And since habitual reactions are often based upon personal choices, these predilections can usually be justified or rejected in the same way that likes and dislikes are.

This brings us back to the type of moral standard that Santayana proposed. He said that people should follow whatever course of action contributes to a network of experiences, ideally an entire lifetime, that will be for them as satisfying as possible. At an earlier stage of the argument, I refused to content myself with a wholly quantitative principle, as this one seems to be, but I failed to supply the qualitative restrictions. Now, however, we may say that an existence that is mindless or trivial or meaningless in terms of what a human being is and can be is inferior regardless of how satisfying it is.

Even the greatest excitement or most intense enjoyment is not necessarily best. A life of emotional orgy would not be most desirable, however great its degree of satisfaction. It would tend to throttle affective as well as cognitive possibilities that are contrary to it, and this would prevent us from achieving aesthetic completeness. A life most worth living would surely be a life that harmonizes, so that it can be aesthetic in its totality, the most satisfying intellectual, emotional, and sensory experiences that a person can have, given what it is to be a human being in the world as it actually is.

Adhering to this standard, people who have to choose among critics, or decide which interests and discriminatory powers they should develop, would consider the implications in terms of future possibilities of consummation. It will not do merely to suggest that they broaden their taste and increase their perceptive abilities. Since most of us make so little use of our capacities, that advice is sound, of course. But it is equally important to recognize that new interests often drive out the old ones and that a person who becomes more critical may also become more intolerant of imperfections. Great art can spoil our enjoyment of lesser art. The man who loves Bach's music may not sneer at the works of Albinoni, but his listening hours are limited, and the more he devotes himself to Bach

the less time he will have for composers he deems inferior. Albinoni will have to suffer, which is a shame. The individual's choice
can be justified if, in the long run, he or she can count on Bach for
a totality of richer and more diversified satisfactions. But this does
not diminish the inevitable loss.

I offer this analysis only as a tentative means to elucidate, and to
amplify, Santayana's approach. I have said nothing about duty, justice, and the demands of society. Nevertheless, the standard I have
sketched may help to clarify the way in which an entire lifetime can
become a great and significant work of art. Living a good life is a
kind of experiential art form. Arts such as music, painting, poetry,
sculpture are morally justifiable to the extent that they further experience that is, for some person, the best of which he or she is
capable. A priori, the "fine" arts are not to be ranked higher than
any other kind of art. But as a matter of fact, they tend to make an
outstanding contribution toward an existence that, for most people,
would be eminently valuable. Above all, they are structurally indicative of what it is to have a life worth living.

In trying to justify the fine arts in this fashion, I am disagreeing
with Santayana's claim that they are innocent, detached from practical concerns, or uniquely liberal. They are not innocent: for they focus experience, making it intense at the same time as it has direction,
rewarding as well as meaningful. They teach us how to perceive. They
may also teach us lies, but they strengthen our grip on the world by
allowing us to enjoy even the wildest misconceptions. They are not
detached from practical concerns: for they change our way of seeing
things and thereby alter our goals and aspirations. They register emotions and can also arouse them in ways that have immediate consequences. All of the greatest art stimulates feeling in order to carry it

through an explicit and consummatory development. What otherwise might have been dissipated and lost is now re-created and its mere occurrence redeemed by aesthetic employment. Nor is art unable to reform the world. Whether or not it leads to direct action, which it occasionally does, its very ability to enliven and to educate gives it a kind of practical efficacy. Through its own contrivances, art attaches us affectively to the world in which we are immersed.

Finally, we must reject the notion that art is uniquely liberal: for there is no servile process to be contrasted with what Santayana calls the ideality of fine art. Any activity and every type of production can be simultaneously useful and artistic, and therefore fine as well as servile. Nor does art play with shadows, doing with appearance what nature does with substance, as Santayana's doctrine of essences would seem to imply. A work of art is an imaginative reconstruction of the world. It not only represents reality but also augments and transforms it creatively.[25]

At times Santayana clearly states that an interest in what he calls fine art ought to be harmonized with other interests, and that works of (fine) art should be useful as well as aesthetic. But once we recognize that fine art cannot be distinguished from servile art in the way that Santayana suggests, we have no need to insist upon unification of a special sort. It makes sense, however, to point out—as Santayana often does—that there are more fine arts than those that aesthetes have traditionally favored.[26]

Like the pragmatists, Santayana uses his ideas about the nature of criticism to establish the importance of pluralism in both aesthetics and morality. He always hews to that. It is a great strength in all his theorizing. We in the twenty-first century may try to go beyond Santayana's philosophy, and as a pluralist he expects us to do so. But even when we move in other directions, as I have done, we can be grateful for what he provides. He has shown our generation how we may proceed.

Epilogue

SINCE THIS BOOK began with an account of my visit to Santayana, a few concluding remarks about the consequences of that visit may be apropos. My increased acquaintance with Santayana's philosophy started when I returned to Harvard. Having written my undergraduate thesis on Dewey's theory of value, I thought that for the time being, at least, I had exhausted my store of ideas about American pragmatism. It continued to influence my formation as a thinker, but I did not want to write a doctoral dissertation that dealt with the problems it examines and creates. Analytic philosophy and Continental existentialism also intrigued me without eliciting a need to carry out, in any detailed manner, the programs they projected.

I veered toward Santayana because he was the first great aesthetician in the history of American philosophy. Despite our differences, I was convinced that Santayana's humanistic works were worthy of the closest attention. Having read his major books, I could see how they renewed the attack on previous philosophies that pragmatism also rejected. The fact that Santayana was a critic of both James and Dewey, and often severe in his censure, seemed secondary to me. In the dissertation that I finally finished, I tried to show how much he resembled the very pragmatists whose views he strenuously opposed. I also claimed that pragmatism was often liable to the same kind of difficulties that I detected in Santayana. The pragmatists were not Neoplatonists like him, but they too retained vestiges of traditional thinking that I considered flawed and unprofitable.

In later years I sometimes sought to distance myself from the study of Santayana. I feared that, even as a critic of his, I ran the risk of being deflected from speaking in my own voice and singing my own song as best as I could. Only recently have I come to appreciate how and why Santayana has had such unremitting importance for me, whether I am basically an imitator or a separate spirit seeking an autonomous self-expression. In either event, Santayana served as a model of the literary philosopher trying to overcome his alienation from a world that has become increasingly oblivious of its need for the humanities.

Although I disagree with Santayana on technical points, I now perceive how helpful his philosophy can be for those who study it fifty years after his death. In my case, his writings provided the blueprint of an outlook that I had only to modify to suit my own sense of reality. If I speak with a somewhat different intonation, I never-theless know that this might not have happened if I had not had his in mind during each phase of my intellectual maturation. In the his-tory of philosophy no one has written about imagination with greater profundity than Santayana.[1] And though his attempt to unify Platonism and naturalism may not be entirely defensible, as I have suggested in this book, his writings always probe the possibilities of an authentic and wholesome harmonization between these two perspectives. The concept of harmony is the leitmotif that resonates in every book of his. As Dewey also did, he recognized the value of philosophy that delineates a significant harmony between nature and spirit in the hope that human beings can thereby work out their destiny with insight and personal success.

Whether or not I am right in arguing that Santayana's mode of distinguishing between nature and spirit perpetuates his residual sense of alienation, and thus prevents him from effecting in his phi-losophy the harmony that he sought, his creativity in the literary presentation of this philosophy excels as only great art does. The world in which we now exist needs such aesthetic achievements more than ever before. Having lived so long with Santayana's as a constant resource, I feel that my pilgrimage to Rome that summer was not in vain.

Notes

PREFACE

1. The video appeared in English as *George Santayana: Spanish Philosopher and Poet,* in Spanish as *George Santayana: Filósofo y Poeta Español* (Bala Cynwyd, Penn.: Schlessinger Video, 1995).

ONE: A PILGRIMAGE TO SANTAYANA

This chapter first appeared in *The Hudson Review* 53, no. 2.

1. George Santayana, *Scepticism and Animal Faith: Introduction to a System of Philosophy* (New York: Scribner's, 1923), p. v.

2. On Santayana in relation to "The Crisis of Western Humanism," see Noël O'Sullivan, *Thinkers of Our Time: Santayana* (St. Albans, England: Claridge, 1992), pp. 23–48. For writings about Santayana, on this and related topics, and originally in languages other than English, see also *Santayana Abroad: The Reception of Santayana's Philosophy in Europe, Latin America, Africa, and Asia,* ed. and trans. supervised by David Wapinsky and Zechariah Switzky (New York: Philanthropica for Public Libraries, 1993).

3. W. Somerset Maugham, *A Writer's Notebook* (Garden City: Doubleday, 1949), p. 341.

4. John Crowe Ransom, "Art and Mr. Santayana," in *Animal Faith and Spiritual Life: Previously Unpublished and Uncollected Writings by George*

Santayana with Critical Essays on his Thought, ed. John Lachs (New York: Appleton-Century-Crofts, 1967), p. 403.

5. *The Letters of George Santayana,* ed. Daniel Cory (New York: Scribner's, 1955), p. 40.

6. George Santayana, *Reason in Common Sense* (New York: Scribner's, 1905), p. 218.

7. George Santayana, *The Sense of Beauty: Being the Outlines of Aesthetic Theory,* ed. William G. Holzberger and Herman J. Saatkamp, Jr. (Cambridge: MIT Press, 1988), p. 49.

8. Ibid., pp. 88, 20. On this, see M. M. Kirkwood, *Santayana: Saint of the Imagination* (Toronto: University of Toronto Press, 1961), pp. 65–79 and passim. See also Willard E. Arnett, *Santayana and the Sense of Beauty* (Gloucester, Mass.: Peter Smith, 1969), pp. 58–81.

9. Henry David Aiken, "George Santayana: Natural Historian of Symbolic Forms," in his *Reason and Conduct: New Bearings in Moral Philosophy* (New York: Knopf, 1962), pp. 315–48; Walter Jackson Bate, *Criticism: The Major Texts* (New York: Harcourt, Brace, 1970), pp. 652–56.

10. Richard Colton Lyon, Preface to *Santayana on America: Essays, Notes, and Letters on American Life, Literature, and Philosophy* (New York: Harcourt, Brace, and World, 1968), p. vi.

11. Gore Vidal, *Palimpsest: A Memoir* (New York: Random House, 1995), p. 159.

12. George Santayana, *The Realm of Essence,* in *Realms of Being* (New York: Scribner's, 1942), p. xiv.

13. Henry James, "The Art of Fiction," in his *Literary Criticism,* 2 vols. (New York: Library of America, 1984), 1:53.

TWO: HIS HOST THE WORLD

Now considerably revised, material in this chapter appeared in *The Hudson Review* 7, no. 3:356–72, and in *New York Review of Books* 1, no. 3:15.

1. George Santayana, *Persons and Places: Fragments of Autobiography,* ed. William G. Holzberger and Herman J. Saatkamp, Jr. (Cambridge: MIT Press, 1986), p. 464.

2. Ibid., p. 539.

3. T. E. Hulme, *Speculations* (London: Routledge and Kegan Paul, 1936), p. 71.

4. On Santayana's influence on Eliot's thinking, particularly about the objective correlative, see B. R. McElderry, Jr., "Santayana and Eliot's 'Objective Correlative,'" *Boston University Studies in English* 3:179–81.

5. George Santayana, "A Brief History of My Opinions," in *The Philosophy of Santayana*, ed. Irwin Edman (New York: Scribner's, 1953), p. 6.

6. Quoted in John McCormick, *George Santayana: A Biography* (New York: Knopf, 1987), p. 97. On Eliot's letter and its circumstances, see also an earlier biography: George W. Howgate, *George Santayana* (New York: A. S. Barnes, 1961), pp. 42–43.

7. Santayana, *Persons and Places*, p. 477.

8. Ibid., p. 429.

9. Santayana, *The Realm of Essence*, in *Realms of Being*, p. 65. For a recent reconsideration of these alternatives in Santayana's thought, see Angus Kerr-Lawson, "Spirit Within a Life of Reason," *Bulletin of the Santayana Society*, no. 16:35–38.

10. *The Philosophy of George Santayana*, ed. Paul Arthur Schilpp, (Evanston: Northwestern University Press, 1940), p. 27. For further discussion, see Chapter 8 of the present book. See also Louis Harap, "A Note on Moralities in the Philosophy of Santayana," in Santayana, *Animal Faith and Spiritual Life*, pp. 359–65.

11. George Santayana, *The Last Puritan: A Memoir in the Form of a Novel*, ed. William G. Holzberger and Herman J. Saatkamp, Jr. (Cambridge: MIT Press, 1994), p. 552. Hereafter in this book, page numbers for quotations from this edition of *The Last Puritan* will appear in parentheses in my text.

12. Blaise Pascal, *Pensées* (New York: Modern Library, 1941), no. 323, p. 109.

13. Henry James, *The Portrait of a Lady* (New York: Viking, 1996), p. 197.

14. Santayana, *Persons and Places*, p. 418.

15. Ibid., p. 511.

16. Daniel Cory, *Santayana, the Later Years: A Portrait with Letters* (New York: Braziller, 1963).

17. Ibid., p. 142.

18. Ibid., pp. 182, 222, 180, 158.

19. Ibid., p. 323.

20. George Santayana, *The Realm of Spirit*, in *Realms of Being*, p. 774.

21. Cory, *Santayana, the Later Years*, p. 324.

22. Ibid., p. 325.

THREE: *THE LAST PURITAN*

This chapter is a much enlarged and somewhat revised version of my introduction to the critical edition of *The Last Puritan* cited above.

1. *The Letters of George Santayana*, p. 190.
2. Ibid., p. 303.
3. *Dialogue on George Santayana*, ed. Corliss Lamont (New York: Horizon, 1959), p. 52.
4. Ibid., pp. 60–61.
5. Santayana, *The Sense of Beauty*, p. 113.
6. Ibid.
7. *The Letters of George Santayana*, p. 306.
8. John Dewey, "Santayana's Novel," in *John Dewey: The Later Works, 1925– 1953*, ed. Jo Ann Boydston (Carbondale: Southern Illinois University Press, 1987), 2:446.
9. *The Letters of George Santayana*, p. 302.
10. Ralph Barton Perry, *Puritanism and Democracy* (New York: Vanguard, 1944), p. 64.
11. *Dialogue on George Santayana*, p. 60.
12. William James, *Essays on Faith and Morals* (New York: New American Library, 1974), p. 258.
13. *The Letters of George Santayana*, p. 410.
14. *The Philosophy of Santayana*, 569–70.
15. *The Letters of George Santayana*, p. 302.
16. Ibid., p. 308.
17. Ibid., p. 305.
18. Cory, *Santayana, the Later Years*, pp. 40–41.
19. Ibid., p. 43.
20. Ibid., p. 163.
21. Santayana, *Persons and Places*, in particular pp. 291–320.
22. Santayana, *Reason in Society*, pp. 155–56.
23. For a discussion of Renoir's film, see my book *Reality Transformed: Film as Meaning and Technique* (Cambridge: MIT Press, 1998), pp. 155–89.
24. *The Letters of George Santayana*, p. 208.
25. Santayana, *The Realm of Spirit*, in *Realms of Being*, pp. 791 ff. See also *The Letters of George Santayana*, p. 331.
26. Sigmund Freud, *The Standard Edition of the Complete Psychological Works of Sigmund Freud* (London: Hogarth Press and the Institute of Psycho-

Analysis, 1957 et seq.) 11:177–90. Freud's complete works are hereafter cited as *SE.*

27. George Santayana to Charles P. Davis, April 3, 1936. Quoted in McCormick, *George Santayana,* p. 336.

28. George Santayana, *Essays in Literary Criticism,* ed. Irving Singer, New York: Scribner's, 1956), p. 222. On Santayana's "festive criticism" and "comic faith," see Henry Samuel Levinson, *Santayana, Pragmatism, and the Spiritual Life* (Chapel Hill: University of North Carolina Press, 1992), pp. 197–203, 231–33, and passim. See also Elkin Calhoun Wilson, *Shakespeare, Santayana, and the Comic* (University: University of Alabama Press, 1973), pp. 7–26.

29. Santayana, "Ultimate Religion," in *The Philosophy of Santayana,* p. 581. See also Santayana's essay "The Ethical Doctrine of Spinoza," in George Santayana, *The Idler and His Works, and Other Essays,* ed. Daniel Cory (New York: George Braziller, 1957), particularly pp. 82–83. On the importance for Santayana of Spinoza's thought, see H. T. Kirby-Smith, *A Philosophical Novelist: George Santayana and* The Last Puritan (Carbondale: Southern Illinois University Press, 1997), pp. 26–48.

30. For additional writings about the novel, see Kirby-Smith, *A Philosophical Novelist,* particularly pp. 113–68; Levinson, *Santayana, Pragmatism, and the Spiritual Life,* pp. 242–48; Anthony Woodward, *Living in the Eternal: A Study of George Santayana* (Nashville: Vanderbilt University Press, 1988), pp. 128–49; Joel Porte, *Representative Man: Ralph Waldo Emerson in His Time* (New York: Oxford University Press, 1979), pp. 16–31; Henny Wenkart, "The Primordial Myth of the Bad Mother and the Good Mother in *Persons and Places* and in *The Last Puritan,*" *Bulletin of the Santayana Society* 10:9–16; Daniel Aaron, "Postscript to *The Last Puritan,*" *New England Quarterly* 9:683–86; and the following essays in *Critical Essays on George Santayana,* ed. Kenneth M. Price and Robert C. Leitz, III (Boston: G. K. Hall, 1992): William H. Marshall, "An Expanding Theme in *The Last Puritan,*" pp. 100–109; James C. Ballowe, "*The Last Puritan* and the Failure in American Culture," pp. 127–38; William G. Holzberger, "The Significance of the Subtitle of Santayana's Novel *The Last Puritan: A Memoir in the Form of a Novel,*" pp. 232–55; Peter Conn, "Paternity and Patriarchy: *The Last Puritan* and the 1930s," pp. 272–89; and three short pieces, each entitled "*The Last Puritan,*" by Ellen Glasgow, Richard Church, and Conrad Aiken respectively, pp. 28–41.

FOUR: IDEALIZATION: SANTAYANA VERSUS FREUD

Material in this chapter and the one that follows it first appeared, in an earlier version, in the first and third volumes of my *Nature of Love* trilogy.

1. George Santayana, *Reason in Society* (New York: Dover, 1980), p. 31.
2. Ibid.
3. Ibid., p. 91.
4. Freud, *On Narcissism: An Introduction*, in *SE*, 14:94.
5. Freud, *Three Essays on Sexuality*, in *SE*, 7:150.
6. Freud, *Group Psychology and the Analysis of the Ego*, in *SE*, 18:112.
7. Freud, *On Narcissism*, in *SE*, 14:88.
8. Freud, "The Resistances to Psycho-Analysis," in *SE*, 19:218.
9. Freud, "A Special Type of Choice of Object Made by Man," in *SE*, 11:169.
10. Santayana, *Reason in Society*, p. 91.
11. George Santayana, *Interpretations of Poetry and Religion*, ed. William G. Holzberger and Herman J. Saatkamp, Jr. (Cambridge: MIT Press, 1989), p. 79.
12. For a presentation of my distinction between appraisal and bestowal, see my trilogy *The Nature of Love*, particularly vol. 1, *Plato to Luther* (Chicago: University of Chicago Press, 1984), pp. 3–22, and vol. 3, *The Modern World* (Chicago: University of Chicago Press, 1987), pp. 390–406. For further discussion of Santayana's thinking in relation to Freud's, see Morris Grossman, "Santayana as Dramatist and Dialectician," Ph.D. diss., Columbia University, 1960, pp. 33–48.
13. Santayana, *Reason in Society*, p. 31.

FIVE: SANTAYANA'S PHILOSOPHY OF LOVE

1. George Santayana, *The German Mind: A Philosophical Diagnosis* (New York: Crowell, 1968), p. 119.
2. Santayana, *The Sense of Beauty*, p. 40.
3. Ibid., pp. 41, 42. See also Santayana's discussion of Stendhal's *De l'Amour* in *Persons and Places*, pp. 428–29.
4. Ibid.
5. *The Philosophy of Santayana*, p. 566.
6. Ibid., p. 570.
7. Santayana, *Reason in Society*, p. 11.
8. Ibid., pp. 16, 21.

9. On this dynamic, see James on instinct, in his *The Principles of Psychology* (Cambridge: Harvard University Press, 1981), 2:1004–57.

10. Santayana, *Reason in Society,* p. 9.

11. Ibid.

12. Santayana, *The Realm of Spirit,* in *Realms of Being,* p. 569.

13. Ibid., pp. 572, 549, 636.

14. Ibid., p. 572.

15. Ibid., p. 575.

16. Ibid., p. 548.

17. Santayana, *Reason in Society,* pp. 33, 31.

18. Santayana, *The Realm of Spirit,* in *Realms of Being,* p. 641.

19. Ibid.

20. Ibid., p. 642.

21. Ibid., p. 669.

22. Ibid.

23. See Santayana, *Persons and Places,* p. 429.

24. On the distinction between love of things and love of ideals, see my book *The Pursuit of Love* (Baltimore: Johns Hopkins University Press, 1994), particularly pp. 31–44.

25. For James's remark, see *The Selected Letters of William James,* ed. Elizabeth Hardwick (New York: Farrar, Straus, and Cudahy, 1961), p. 183. For Santayana's comment on James's remark, see Santayana, "On My Friendly Critics," in *Soliloquies in England and Later Soliloquies* (New York: Scribner's, 1922), pp. 247–48. See also Timothy L. S. Sprigge, *Santayana: An Examination of his Philosophy,* rev. and enlarged ed. (London: Routledge, 1995), p. 225, n. 38.

26. Santayana, *Interpretations of Poetry and Religion,* p. 88.

27. Santayana, *Persons and Places,* p. 428. Italics deleted from first sentence.

28. Santayana, *The Realm of Essence,* in *Realms of Being,* p. 16.

29. Ibid. Santayana's kinship to Proust is also evident in his discussion of "the illusion and revelation of the grand passion." He emphasizes the "madness in this devotion" but also remarks: "And yet what soul that has ever known a great love would wish not to have known it?" (Santayana, *The Realm of Spirit,* in *Realms of Being,* pp. 687–88). See also references in Chapter 6, n. 30.

30. *Obiter Scripta: Lectures, Essays and Reviews by George Santayana,* ed. Justus Buchler and Benjamin Schwartz (New York: Scribner's, 1936), pp. 80–81.

31. Santayana, *The Realm of Spirit,* in *Realms of Being,* p. 782.

32. Ibid., p. 820.
33. Ibid., p. 821.
34. Ibid., p. 685.
35. Ibid., p. 686.
36. Ibid., pp. 687, 691–92.
37. Donald C. Williams, in his "Of Essence and Existence and Santayana," in *Animal Faith and Spiritual Life*, pp. 137–38. On Santayana as a "Catholic atheist," see also Santayana, *The Realm of Spirit*, in *Realms of Being*, p. 838, where he says "my philosophy is atheistic"; and John Lachs, *George Santayana* (Boston: Twayne, 1988), pp. 25–26.
38. George Santayana, *Dialogues in Limbo* (New York: Scribner's, 1925), p. 155.
39. Ibid., pp. 139, 156–57.
40. Ibid., p. 158.
41. Santayana, *The Realm of Spirit*, in *Realms of Being*, p. 792.
42. George Santayana, *Platonism and the Spiritual Life*, in *Winds of Doctrine and Platonism and the Spiritual Life* (Gloucester, England: Peter Smith, 1971), pp. 310–11.
43. For further discussion of Santayana on charity and religious love in general, see my book *The Nature of Love: Plato to Luther*, pp. 334–35, 358–59, and passim. See also George Santayana, *Dominations and Powers: Reflections on Liberty, Society, and Government* (New York: Scribner's, 1954), pp. 366–70.
44. Santayana, *The Realm of Spirit*, in *Realms of Being*, p. 773.
45. Ibid., p. 807.
46. Ibid., p. 825.
47. Ibid. For a critique of Santayana's conception of spirit, see my book *The Harmony of Nature and Spirit* (Baltimore: Johns Hopkins University Press, 1996), pp. 160–68 and passim. See also Sprigge, *Santayana*, pp. 107–16. For further discussion of Santayana's ideas about spirit, see Lachs, *George Santayana*, pp. 104–23. See also Woodward, *Living in the Eternal*, pp. 87 ff., 99–119; Levinson, *Santayana, Pragmatism, and the Spiritual Life*, pp. 107–19 and passim; Victorino Tejera, *American Modern: The Path Not Taken* (Lanham, Md.: Rowman and Littlefield, 1996), pp. 83 ff.
48. Santayana, "Friendships," in *Soliloquies in England and Later Soliloquies*, pp. 55–56, 58.
49. Santayana, *Reason in Society*, pp. 148, 156.

50. George Santayana, "Friendship," in *The Birth of Reason and Other Essays*, ed. Daniel Cory (New York: Columbia University Press, 1968), pp. 80–81.

51. Ibid., p. 82.

52. Ibid., pp. 81, 85.

53. Ibid., p. 88.

54. *The Letters of George Santayana*, p. 386.

SIX: SANTAYANA AS A LITERARY CRITIC

An earlier version of this chapter served as the introduction to my edition of Santayana's *Essays in Literary Criticism*.

1. George Santayana, *Three Philosophical Poets: Lucretius, Dante, Goethe* (New York: Cooper Square, 1970), p. v.

2. George Santayana, "Tragic Philosophy," in *Essays in Literary Criticism*, p. 229.

3. Ibid., p. 275. On this, and in relation to my further remarks in the following chapter, see John M. Major, "Santayana on Shakespeare," in *Critical Essays on George Santayana*, pp. 75–86.

4. Santayana, *Three Philosophical Poets*, p. 57.

5. *The Philosophy of George Santayana*, p. 599.

6. Santayana, "A Long Way Round to Nirvana; or Much Ado about Dying," in *The Philosophy of Santayana*, p. 566.

7. Santayana, *Three Philosophical Poets*, p. 120.

8. Santayana, "Dickens," in *Essays in Literary Criticism*, p. 215.

9. *The Philosophy of Santayana*, p. 581.

10. Santayana, *The Last Puritan*, p. 9.

11. Santayana, *Essays in Literary Criticism*, p. 275.

12. Santayana, *Interpretations of Poetry and Religion*, pp. 88, 77.

13. Santayana, *Three Philosophical Poets*, pp. 130, 133.

14. Santayana, *Essays in Literary Criticism*, pp. 191–92.

15. Santayana, *Interpretations of Poetry and Religion*, pp. 108–9.

16. Ibid., p. 104.

17. William Shakespeare, *Hamlet*, act 3, scene 2.

18. Santayana, *Three Philosophical Poets*, p. 203.

19. T. S. Eliot, "Four Quartets," *Collected Poems, 1909–1962* (New York: Harcourt, Brace, and World, 1970), p. 176.

20. Santayana, *Three Philosophical Poets*, pp. 203, 206.

21. Santayana, *Essays in Literary Criticism*, p. 135.

22. For further critical discussion of Santayana's ideas about the relevant questions, see Joel Porte, "Santayana's *Interpretations of Poetry and Religion:* An Introduction," in Santayana, *Interpretations of Poetry and Religion,* pp. xiii–xxxi, particularly pp. xvi–xxii.
23. Santayana, *The Sense of Beauty,* p. 79.
24. Ibid., p. 144.
25. Ibid., p. 113.
26. Santayana, *Interpretations of Poetry and Religion,* p. 3.
27. Santayana, *The Sense of Beauty,* pp. 119, 117.
28. George Santayana, *Reason in Art* (New York: Scribner's, 1905), p. 112.
29. Santayana, *Three Philosophical Poets,* p. 11.
30. Santayana, "Proust on Essences," in *Essays in Literary Criticism,* p. 241. On Santayana in relation to Proust, see Van Meter Ames, *Proust and Santayana: The Aesthetic Way of Life* (Chicago: Willett, Clark, 1937), pp. 49–80. See also my criticism of Santayana's interpretation of Proust on essence in my book *The Nature of Love: The Modern World,* pp. 210–14.
31. See Irving Singer, *Santayana's Aesthetics: A Critical Introduction* (Cambridge: Harvard University Press, 1957). For a study of Santayana's doctrine of essence, see Sprigge, *Santayana,* pp. 65–94; and Kirby-Smith, *A Philosophical Novelist,* pp. 49–66.
32. George Santayana, "The Mutability of Esthetic Categories," *The Philosophical Review* 34, no. 3: 284 n; also included in "An Aesthetic Soviet," in *Obiter Scripta,* p. 255.
33. Santayana, "On My Friendly Critics," in *Soliloquies in England and Later Soliloquies,* pp. 254–55.

SEVEN: GREATNESS IN ART

Material in this chapter and the one that follows it first appeared in an earlier, and now much revised, version in my book *Santayana's Aesthetics: A Critical Introduction,* cited above.
1. Santayana, *Interpretations of Poetry and Religion,* p. 154.
2. Ibid.
3. Ibid., p. 155.
4. Ibid., p. 109.
5. Santayana, *Winds of Doctrine: Studies in Contemporary Opinion,* in *Winds of Doctrine and Platonism and the Spiritual Life,* p. 203.
6. Santayana, *Three Philosophical Poets,* p. 58.

7. Santayana, *Interpretations of Poetry and Religion*, p. 108.

8. Santayana, *Essays in Literary Criticism*, p. 238.

9. Santayana, *Interpretations of Poetry and Religion*, pp. 158–59.

10. Santayana, *Three Philosophical Poets*, p. 59.

11. Santayana, *Interpretations of Poetry and Religion*, pp. 161, 168–69.

12. Ibid., p. 95.

13. Santayana, *Essays in Literary Criticism*, p. 135.

14. Santayana, *Three Philosophical Poets*, pp. 8, 10, 11.

15. Santayana, *Reason in Art*, p. 112.

16. Santayana, *Three Philosophical Poets*, p. 204.

17. Ibid., p. 207.

18. Santayana, *Essays in Literary Criticism*, pp. 200, 197.

19. Santayana, *Three Philosophical Poets*, p. 133.

20. Ibid., pp. 211, 213, 25.

21. Santayana, *Soliloquies in England and Later Soliloquies*, pp. 254–55.

22. Santayana, *Reason in Art*, p. 122.

23. Santayana, *Soliloquies in England and Later Soliloquies*, p. 255.

24. Santayana, *Interpretations of Poetry and Religion*, p. 117.

25. Santayana, *Essays in Literary Criticism*, p. 269.

26. For discussion of various topics in this and the following chapter, see Jerome Ashmore, *Santayana, Art, and Aesthetics* (Cleveland: Press of Western Reserve University, 1966), pp. 7–69 in particular; and Arnett, *Santayana and the Sense of Beauty*, pp. 135–81.

EIGHT: THE BASIS OF AESTHETIC AND MORAL CRITICISM

1. Santayana, *Obiter Scripta*, p. 37.

2. Santayana, *The Sense of Beauty*, p. 29.

3. Ibid., p. 30.

4. Santayana, *Reason in Art*, pp. 194, 195.

5. Ibid., p. 197.

6. Ibid., p. 202.

7. Ibid., pp. 169, 170.

8. Ibid., pp. 172, 173.

9. Ibid., p. 175.

10. Ibid., p. 229.

11. Santayana, *Obiter Scripta*, p. 38.

12. Santayana, *Reason in Art*, p. 210.

13. Santayana, *The Sense of Beauty*, pp. 136, 137.

14. *The Philosophy of George Santayana*, p. 578.

15. Milton Karl Munitz, *The Moral Philosophy of Santayana*, (New York: Columbia University Press, 1953), p. 88.

16. *The Philosophy of George Santayana*, p. 563; Santayana, *Platonism and the Spiritual Life*, p. 258; *The Philosophy of George Santayana*, pp. 584–85.

17. Santayana, *Dominations and Powers*, p. 128, 40 n.

18. Ibid., p. 313.

19. Ibid.

20. I presented this argument in *John Dewey's Theory of Value*, Widener Archives, Harvard University, 1948. On Dewey and the pragmatists in relation to Santayana, see Levinson, *Santayana, Pragmatism, and the Spiritual Life*, pp. 1–8, 218–21, and 251–56.

21. Bertrand Russell, "The Philosophy of Santayana," in *The Philosophy of George Santayana*, p. 465.

22. On Santayana's ethical theory, see Willard E. Arnett, *George Santayana* (New York: Washington Square, 1968), pp. 108–23; Sprigge, *Santayana*, pp. 188–208; and Beth J. Singer, *The Rational Society: A Critical Study of Santayana's Social Thought* (Cleveland: Press of Case Western Reserve University, 1970), pp. 59–120.

23. Stephen C. Pepper, *The Basis of Criticism in the Arts* (Cambridge: Harvard University Press, 1946), p. 52.

24. Santayana, *Three Philosophical Poets*, p. 133.

25. I develop this approach much further in my book *The Harmony of Nature and Spirit*, particularly pp. 96–144.

26. I enlarge on this idea, in relation to Santayana's speculations about the ontology of the photographic image, in my book *Reality Transformed*, pp. 31–37 and passim. See George Santayana, "The Photograph and the Mental Image," in *Animal Faith and Spiritual Life*, pp. 391–403. See also my article "Santayana and the Ontology of the Photographic Image," *The Journal of Aesthetics and Art Criticism* 36, no. 1:39–43.

EPILOGUE

1. For collateral corroboration of this claim, see Lucy Beckett, "Imagination as Value," in *Critical Essays on George Santayana*, pp. 174–92.

Index

Index